THE Crystal EXPERIENCE

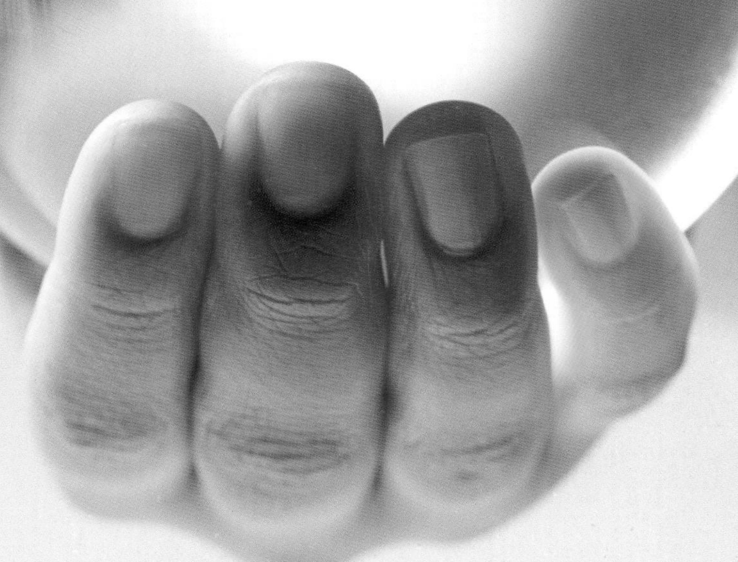

THE

Crystal

EXPERIENCE

your complete crystal workshop

Judy Hall

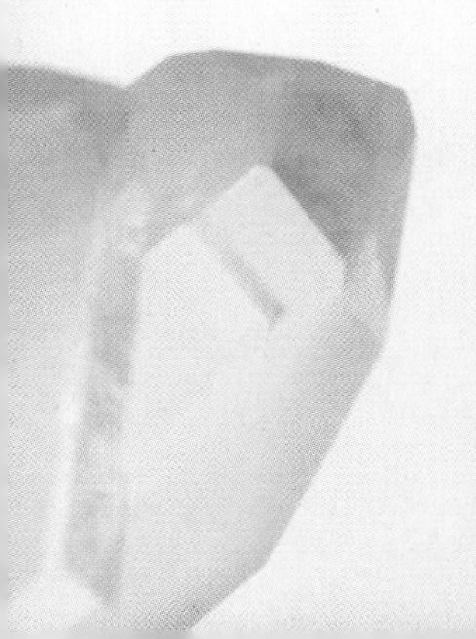

This edition published in 2021 by Pyramid,
an imprint of Octopus Publishing Group Ltd
Carmelite House
50 Victoria Embankment
London EC4Y 0DZ
www.octopusbooks.co.uk

First published in Great Britain in 2010 by
Godsfield, a division of Octopus Publishing Group Ltd
An Hachette UK Company
www.hachette.co.uk

Reprinted in 2014 and 2015

ISBN 978-0-753734-31-5

10 9 8 7 6 5 4 3 2 1

A CIP catalogue record for this book is
available from the British Library

Printed and bound in China

No medical claims are made for the stones in this book and the information given is not intended to act as a substitute for medical treatment. If you are in any doubt about their use, a qualified crystal-healing practitioner should be consulted. In the context of this book, illness is thought of as a 'dis-ease', the final manifestation of spiritual, environmental, psychological, karmic, emotional or mental imbalance or distress. Healing means bringing mind, body and spirit back into balance and facilitating evolution for the soul, it does not imply a cure. In accordance with crystal-healing consensus, all stones are referred to as crystals, regardless of whether or not they have a crystalline structure.

The audio material for this workshop is available from library.guidedwellbeing.app or from the Guided Wellbeing Library app.

CONTENTS

Introduction 8

How to use the book and audio 12

Building up a picture 12

Glossary of terms 15

How do I choose a crystal? 17

What's in my collection? 18

Choosing a crystal 20

Cleansing, activating and storing crystals 22

Which crystals will I need? 24

Crystal directory 26

Choosing and cleansing exercises 33

EXERCISE 1: Identifying my crystals 34

EXERCISE 2: What do my fingers tell me? 40

EXERCISE 3: The big crystal cleanse 42

EXERCISE 4: Attuning to my crystals 44

All about crystals 49

What is a crystal? 50

Do shape and colour matter? 52

Crystal systems 62

Shape and colour exercises 65

EXERCISE 5: Feel me 66

EXERCISE 6: Which colour am I? 70

EXERCISE 7: Which shape am I? 74

EXERCISE 8: What system do I belong to? 78

Crystals and the chakras 81

Chakras and healing 82

Chakras and colour 88

Chakras and the aura 90

Opening the higher chakras 92

Chakra exercises 97

EXERCISE 9: Full chakra cleanse, balance and recharge 98

EXERCISE 10: What colour are my chakras? 102

EXERCISE 11: Strengthening my aura 104

EXERCISE 12: Bringing my higher chakras on-line 108

Crystals for self-development 113

Crystal qualities 114

Which crystals do I love? 116

Which crystals do I avoid? 118

How can I protect myself with crystals? 120

Protecting my space 124

Self-development exercises 129

EXERCISE 13: My Quartz crystal journey 130

EXERCISE 14: What do the crystals I love tell me? 134

EXERCISE 15: Facing my shadow energy 138

EXERCISE 16: Protecting my spleen 140

EXERCISE 17: Using grid systems 142

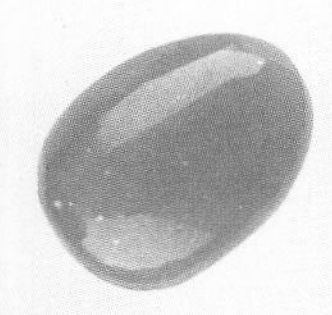

How can I be my own crystal healer? 145

Sources of dis-ease 146
Crystals and my emotions 148
Releasing from the past 150
Crystals and my organs 152
Crystals and my mind 158
Healing exercises 161
EXERCISE 18: Finding my immune-system crystal 162
EXERCISE 19: My Rainbow Obsidian journey 166
EXERCISE 20: My detox layout 170
EXERCISE 21: Improving my mind 174

How do I keep my crystals working? 177

Working with crystals every day 178
Crystal bathing 180
Crystal massage 182
Talking to your crystals 184
Incorporating new spiritual qualities 186
Gem essences 190
Exercises to keep crystals working 193
EXERCISE 22: Travelling my inner planes 194
EXERCISE 23: Giving myself a crystal massage 196
EXERCISE 24: Finding my inner balance 198
EXERCISE 25: Accessing my spiritual gifts 202
EXERCISE 26: Using my gem essence 204

Taking crystal work further 209

Working with higher vibration crystals 210
Crystal rituals and journeys 218
Attracting love 222
Exercises to take crystal work further 225
EXERCISE 27: Comparing my high- and low-vibration crystals 226
EXERCISE 28: Attuning to my high-vibration crystals 228
EXERCISE 29: My Attracting Love Ritual 232
EXERCISE 30: My Wholeness Meditation 236

Inspirations (audio scripts) 241

TRACK 1: Relaxation, focusing and opening the mind's eye 242
TRACK 2: Attuning to my crystals 244
TRACK 4: The Quartz crystal journey 246
TRACK 5: The Rainbow Obsidian journey 248

Index 250

Acknowledgements 256

Audio tracks

TRACK 1: Relaxation, focusing and opening the mind's eye
TRACK 2: Attuning to my crystals
TRACK 3: Music only
TRACK 4: The Quartz crystal journey
TRACK 5: The Rainbow Obsidian journey

Introduction

Have you ever wanted to get up close and personal with your crystals? To become totally attuned to them? Have you read a book about crystal properties and thought I'd so like to know more, to really experience this for myself? Well, now you can. My books *The Crystal Bible volume 1* and *volume 2* describe in detail the attributes of almost five hundred crystals and their healing properties. This book is different. Rather than telling you what each crystal does, it helps you to discover for yourself how you respond to a particular crystal and what that crystal has to offer you. It is exactly like attending a workshop with me to explore how you can work with crystals for self-healing and personal development *in the right way for you.*

In my workshops, I don't tell people what to do or what to expect. Instead I encourage them to experience a crystal for themselves by opening their minds to exciting possibilities and playing joyfully with the wondrous little beings that are crystals. I know that everybody is unique and everyone experiences the energy of a particular crystal differently because of personal expectations, past experiences, energetic overlays, emotional blocks, environmental factors and the effects of spiritual practices.

Some of my most potent crystal remedies have come about through what I call serendipitious synchronicity – the right crystals happened to be there at the right time. In one workshop, for example, a surprisingly large Stibnite wand sat in front of me alongside a huge Chlorite Quartz long point, both recently purchased, plus a beloved piece of Selenite that also formed a wand. When I put these crystals on the table I had no idea what I would use them for. But when I suddenly needed a portal to help lost souls depart this world and go to the light, I picked up the three crystals and held them one on top of the other. This created an extremely efficient portal, and many smaller versions are now in use all over the world. Similarly, I intuitively used Vivianite to heal an extremely sore eye before I intellectually knew that this was

an eye crystal, and a Cathedral Quartz took away a nasty backache just weeks before one of my favourite crystal shop owners said, 'I give anyone who comes into the shop with a pain or who feels under the weather one of these to hold and they go out feeling so much better.'

So, this book helps you to find out for yourself exactly which crystals resonate with you. It helps you to explore their subtle energies and vibrations, colours and shapes, and it takes you on journeys deep into the heart of yourself and All That Is. You'll find guidance on choosing crystals, building up a crystal collection and expanding your knowledge, whether you are a beginner or an experienced crystal worker. By taking part in this crystal workshop you will develop your skills in relaxation, visualization and intuition, too. Relaxation involves entering a receptive state of mind in which your attention is focused inward and disregards external stimuli yet remains alert. Visualization means seeing pictures in your mind's eye and taking journeys through your imagination into other ways of being. When you develop your intuition, you pay attention to the subtle messages that your body, mind and environment are sending you all the time but that you may not have noticed up to now.

You will find it helpful to relax, focus and open your mind's eye before undertaking any of the journeys in this book. With practice, this preparation will take only a few moments.

Work with the audio now Track 1
Learn how to relax, focus your intention and open your mind's eye (to follow the script, see pages 242–43). If you would like to listen to the track lying down, place seven Amethysts around your head to create a calm space and an Apophyllite pyramid over your third eye at the centre of your forehead to open your mind's eye.

Throughout this book you will find symbols to guide you into the next stage of your crystal exploration.

This exercise/journey is suitable for Exercises are usually given for a specific crystal, so this symbol tells you which other crystals in your collection you could also use. Journeying with several crystals helps you to establish the differences between them and find exactly the right one for you.

Work with your crystal/s now This symbol guides you to the relevant practical exercise when you are ready, where you will find full instructions to follow.

I'm not quite there yet If you don't yet feel confident about doing the exercise, this symbol gives suggestions for ways to revise and prepare yourself.

Work with the audio now This symbol tells you when to use the audio and which track to select. The audio tracks are available to download from library.guidedwellbeing.com, or from the Guided Wellbeing Library app. If you would like to follow the script to the audio, turn to the pages indicated in the Inspirations chapter on pages 241–249.

How to use the book and audio

This book is divided into different sections that have been specially designed to lead you step-by-step into a deeper energetic understanding of crystals as you gain in experience and confidence.

In the first part of each section you will find a brief introduction to the subject, suggestions of which crystals you could use and directions to guide you to the practical exercises once you feel ready to experience the crystal for yourself. There are also suggestions for what to do if you're not quite ready for the practical experience. At every stage you have the choice to move on or to revise previous work so that you can take things at your own pace and gradually build up your knowledge.

In the second part of each section of the book you will find exercises, guided questions and space to record your experiences and the answers and insights you have discovered. You can read about the properties of the crystals before you work with a crystal, either in *The Crystal Bible* volumes or in the Crystal Directory on pages 26–32. Alternatively, wait until after you have completed a practical exercise to look up the crystal's properties, or simply work with the qualities you discover for yourself. The audio tracks that accompany this book have been devised to guide you into the relaxed, receptive state that best facilitates crystal journeys and experiences. When you play the track recommended for an exercise (as directed by this audio symbol) just follow the instructions you hear. There will be a musical interlude while you carry them out, followed by more instructions guiding you to the next stage of the exercise. If you need further time to practise, pause the track and move on when you are ready. You will also find a music-only tracks to use as an optional background accompaniment to many of the exercises. This lasts for 20 minutes and its ending closes the exercise.

Building up a picture

Recording your insights and experiences is essential if you are to get the most out of this book, and space is provided for you to write your experiences into the book after each exercise. When writing down your observations, remember to record the date and time and the crystal you used. By varying the time you do the exercises, you can find out whether there

is a particular time of day when you are more intuitive or receptive to crystal energies. Some people find it easer to work with crystals in the morning, for instance, and others in the afternoon or evening. If you find there is a significant difference, time your sessions accordingly.

Recording your experiences in the present tense – 'I am walking ... I am hearing ...' and so on – helps you to re-enter more fully into the experience later and recall as much information as possible. Write down even the tiniest, seemingly least significant detail, because it may assume greater importance later. Remember to pay attention to the sensations in your body: the feelings you have, the thoughts that pass through your mind, the sounds or smells you become aware of, how your heart rate and breathing change and, most of all, whether any particular area of your body is affected by the crystal. Part of you might tingle, for example, or become uncomfortable, hot, cold or painful; alternatively, it might feel comforted or soothed.

The journal entries include questions to help you focus on how the crystal affected you, the emotional, mental or energetic changes it brought about and the insights you received about the crystal's properties. Filling these in as fully as possible will help you to monitor your insights and keep track of the ways in which your intuition opens. Don't hesitate to go back and add to the record if you remember something later – but do put the date and time beside it, making it clear that this is an addition to the original record. You might find it helpful to hold the crystal you worked with as you record your insights and then to return to it for several days afterward, sitting quietly and holding the crystal for a few minutes to see if any new insights arise.

Glossary of terms

You will encounter many of these crystal-healing terms as you work through the book; familiarizing yourself with them now will help you to gain more from the exercises.

All That Is

Spirit, the Source, the divine. The sum total of everything that is.

Aura/subtle body

Subtle bio-energetic field surrounding the physical body, which can be sensed intuitively. The aura holds imprints of emotions, blockages, thoughts and injuries.

Cellular memory

Genetic or past-life information encoded into the cells.

Chakra

Linkage point between subtle energy and the physical body. Chakra malfunction leads to physical, emotional, mental and spiritual *dis-ease.*

Crystal

All stones, gems and minerals in their raw state, regardless of whether they have a crystalline structure.

Dis-ease

Final manifestation of spiritual, environmental, psychological, karmic, emotional or mental imbalance or distress.

Etheric blueprint

Subtle energy pattern, programme or grid from which the physical body is constructed. It carries imprints from past lives, previous attitudes, trauma or injury and ancestral beliefs.

Geopathic stress

Negative energy carried by the earth, generated by water, electromagnetic stress and other disturbances.

Grids/gridding/layouts

Placing crystals around yourself or a building to bring about balance, energy enhancement or protection.

Grounding/grounded

Anchoring energies in the earth; being fully connected to your physical body and the earth on which you walk.

Healing

Bringing the body and its subtle energies, mind, spirit and emotions back into balance on all levels. Healing does not imply cure.

Healing challenge

Some crystals may rapidly release underlying causes of *dis-ease*, temporarily worsening a condition
(a catharsis). If this occurs, remove the crystal and rebalance yourself by holding Smoky Quartz or another appropriate crystal.

Higher vibration/resonance

Refined, purer vibration that usually resonates faster. Higher vibrations exist on earth, in the physical body or in other dimensions.

Journeying

When the consciousness leaves day-to-day awareness and travels through various dimensions and locations.

Lightbody

Subtle energy body vibrating at a high frequency. A vehicle for *Spirit*.

Meridians

Subtle energy channels that radiate through the physical body and can be accessed through acupuncture points.

Self

The higher, extended part of you that is not totally incarnated within your physical body and that can therefore access other lives and other dimensions and the totality of your being.

Spirit/Source

See *All That Is*.

Celestite cluster

Onyx ball

HOW DO I CHOOSE A CRYSTAL?

What's in my collection?

It's always handy to keep a selection of crystals ready for use, and the Crystal Directory on pages 26–32 will help you to identify which ones you already have. It will also highlight gaps in your collection.

You can choose either tumbled or raw crystals – and why not have both? Tumbled stones are comfortable to lay on your body, and raw stones can be placed around your environment. You don't have to buy crystals to add to your collection. You can also use crystals that you find in nature, such as Flint, which has been used in healing for thousands of years, or Snow Quartz pebbles from a beach or river. If you have an aversion to certain crystals or colours, turn to pages 118–19 to find out why.

It is wise to collect a selection of colours and shapes (see pages 54–64) because each one has specific properties and chakra associations (see pages 82–88). However, as you work through the book, you are sure to discover other crystals that resonate with you and your chakras.

This exercise is suitable for All the crystals in your current collection.

Work with your crystals now To work out which crystals you have in your collection and what to use them for, turn to Exercise 1: Identifying My Crystals on page 34.

Choosing a crystal

There are three main ways to choose a crystal: rationally, intuitively and by dowsing. All three selection methods work with any crystal. Crystal energy is subtle, but once you are attuned to it and focused you will quickly be able to recognize the right crystal for you. Don't forget to write down all the crystals you choose on pages 35–39.

Choosing a crystal rationally

The rational way to choose a crystal is to look up the property you are seeking in the Crystal Directory on pages 26–32 or in the indexes to *The Crystal Bible* volumes or *Crystal Prescriptions*. Then go into a shop or online and buy the appropriate crystal. However, once you have bought a range of crystals you still need to choose exactly which one to work with on any occasion. To do this it is useful to open your intuition and listen for the crystal that is calling you, or you could try dowsing.

Choosing a crystal intuitively

Allowing a crystal to 'speak' to you involves opening your inner eyes and ears and seeking with your heart rather than your head to find out which crystal would like to be worked with. You can do this at home using your own collection or whenever you're in a crystal shop. First, relax and quieten your mind, then choose the crystal that your eyes first alight on, the one that seems to stick to your fingers or the one you suddenly realize you've been carrying around the shop. When you connect with the crystal's vibration, you may feel your energy jump or tingle – like getting an electric shock – or slow and deepen. It may pulse in your hand or you may actually hear the crystal's note.

This exercise is suitable for Any crystal in your collection or a crystal shop.

Work with your crystals now To explore finger dowsing further, turn to Exercise 2: What Do My Fingers Tell Me? on page 40.

Choosing a crystal by finger dowsing

This is an excellent way to choose a crystal. It harnesses your body's innate ability to tell you what is good for you and what is not.

Begin by looping your thumb and finger together as shown. (Use whichever hand instinctively feels right to you.)

Slip your other thumb and finger through the loop and close them. Hold the loop over a crystal and ask if this one is beneficial for you.

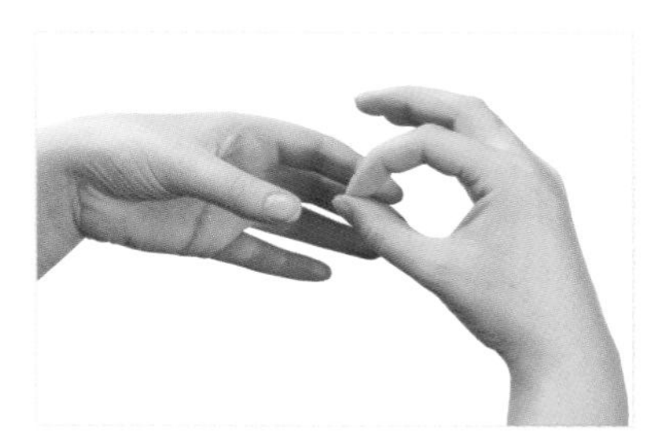

Pull steadily. If the loop breaks, the answer is no. If the loop holds, the answer is yes. Remember to record your results on pages 35–39.

Cleansing, activating and storing crystals

Many people ask why crystals don't work for them and why they feel dragged down rather than uplifted when they handle a crystal. Frequently, this is because the crystal hasn't yet been asked to work or been attuned to the user's unique energy frequency. An even more likely answer is that it hasn't been cleansed before use. Crystals pick up vibrations from everyone who handles them, and they also absorb negative energies. So, if you don't cleanse your crystals you'll pick up bad vibes and won't feel the benefits that a purified crystal can bring you.

Cleansing crystals

You can cleanse and recharge most crystals by holding them under running water for a few minutes and then placing them in the sun for a few hours. Natural water, such as a stream or the sea, is best (put small crystals in a bag to prevent them from being washed away), although you can use tap water. If there is no sun available, visualize bright white light radiating down onto the crystals. It is best to cleanse fragile, layered or friable crystals by placing them in brown rice overnight. They can also be laid on a large Quartz cluster or a Carnelian. White stones enjoy recharging in moonlight. Always cleanse your crystals before and after you use them for healing.

Activating crystals

Close your eyes and concentrate on the crystals. See them surrounded by bright white light. Ask that they be attuned to your own unique frequency and that they be activated to act for your highest good. Ask for the crystals to be blessed by the highest energies in the universe and for them to be dedicated to your own self-healing and the healing of the environment around you.

Storing crystals

A cloth bag is a good place to store tumbled stones, but more delicate stones can be kept wrapped in a cloth or displayed on a shelf. Be aware that crystals that are worn or kept in your environment absorb negative energies and need regular cleansing.

This exercise is suitable for Cleansing is essential for all crystals.

Work with your crystals now To carry out a thorough crystal cleanse and activation, turn to Exercise 3: The Big Crystal Cleanse on pages 42–43.

Which crystals will I need?

I have chosen the crystals in the Crystal Directory on pages 26–32 carefully to cover a wide spectrum of colours and properties and because they are relatively cheap and easy to track down. These make a good collection to begin with. However, do add your own personal favourite crystals to this list; the directory is not intended to be definitive. Once you have assembled and cleansed your crystals (see pages 22–23), you can begin the practical exercises.

As you become more experienced, you might like to work with higher vibration crystals, and these are profiled in a separate directory on pages 212–17. Again, you may attract more of these amazing consciousness-raising beauties to yourself than are profiled on those pages. You need to check out the properties of high-vibration crystals carefully because they tend to be specifically attuned to certain frequencies or vibrations that must mesh with your own energetic emanations. If you don't connect with one crystal, try another and return to the first one later.

This exercise is suitable for Any crystal in your collection.

Work with your crystal now To prepare yourself to spend time with a crystal, turn to Exercise 4: Attuning to My Crystals on page 44.

I'm not quite there yet If you haven't yet learned to cleanse or activate a crystal, turn back to pages 22–23.

CRYSTAL DIRECTORY

Bloodstone (trigonal; red and green)
An excellent all-round healer, Bloodstone stimulates or sedates the immune system as required and has been used for thousands of years to heal the kidneys and blood. Instils courage and selflessness and helps you to act in the present moment.

Halite (cubic; pink, white or blue)
A useful physical and emotional cleanser, Halite assists in spiritual purification and detachment. It brings about metabolic and cellular balance and, ameliorating water retention, is helpful for skin conditions and detoxification. Overcomes anger, abandonment and rejection and instils contentment. Dissolves in water.

Rose Quartz (trigonal; pink)
A crystal of unconditional love and forgiveness, Rose Quartz calms and gently dissolves negativity or grief. The perfect emotional healer, it brings about necessary change and is also excellent for the circulatory and respiratory systems. Instils compassion and empathy and overcomes deprivation.

Garnet (cubic; red, green, orange)
A powerful energizing and regeneration crystal, especially for the chakras, metabolism and libido, Garnet is a sexual stimulant, removing inhibitions. It can also be used for purification and healing the blood and circulation. Releases anger and strengthens the survival instinct.

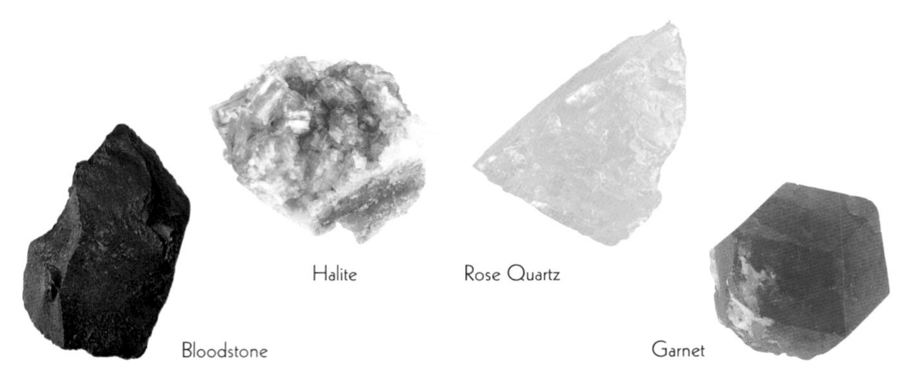

Halite

Rose Quartz

Bloodstone

Garnet

Jasper (trigonal; all colours) Available in a multitude of colours, patterns and forms, Jasper sustains during time of stress and induces tranquillity. It aligns the chakras and facilitates journeying. Traditionally used for protection and to support the circulatory system and the digestive and sexual organs. Encourages assertiveness, organizational skills and self-honesty.

Carnelian (trigonal; red, pink and orange) A crystal of prosperity and vitality, Carnelian helps you to be fully present. A useful protector, especially against other people's rage, it has traditionally been used to support the reproductive organs and circulatory system and to increase fertility. Instils courage, enhances analytic skills and helps you to overcome abuse.

Amber (amorphous; yellowish brown, green) An ancient crystal of healing and protection, Amber is a powerful cleanser and regenerator. It can lift depression and is a useful mental enlivener; it also promotes emotional trust and encourages the body to heal itself. Enhances self-expression and decision-making.

Citrine (trigonal; yellow, smoky) An exceptional attractor of abundance, Citrine also acts as a powerful cleanser and invigorator. This crystal enhances self-esteem and confidence and promotes joy. Excellent for concentration. Enhances creativity and generosity of spirit.

Carnelian

Amber

Blue Jasper

Citrine

Calcite (hexagonal; all colours) A useful purifier, Calcite amplifies energy and alleviates stress. Available in most colours, it promotes emotional intelligence and hopefulness and increases motivation, helping to combat laziness. Instils discernment and serenity.

Aventurine (trigonal; green, blue, peach) Exceptionally useful for blocking geopathic stress and electromagnetic smog, Green Aventurine prevents psychic vampires from pulling on your energy. Aventurine has traditionally been used to attract prosperity and helps you to see alternative possibilities. Instils compassion and leadership qualities and calms anger.

Moss Agate (trigonal; green and blue) A crystal of great stability that encourages fertility, Moss Agate is an excellent all-round energy protector and environmental enhancer. A crystal of new beginnings that strengthens positive personality traits, it has traditionally been used to assist birth. Helps intellectual people to access their feelings and emotional people to gain objectivity.

Malachite (monoclinic; green) Bringing issues and negativity to the surface rapidly, Malachite absorbs environmental and emotional toxins. A crystal of transformation, it assists in inner journeys and mercilessly pinpoints anything blocking spiritual growth. The intensity of Malachite goes to the core of a problem and accesses your shadow. Encourages risk-taking and releases outworn patterns.

Calcite

Aventurine

Moss Agate

Malachite

Peridot (orthorhombic; green) A protective crystal for the aura, Peridot was traditionally believed to repel evil spirits. It is useful for removing old baggage or obsessions and releasing guilt, jealousy and stress. Instils emotional clarity and shows how to forgive yourself.

Jade (monoclinic; all colours) One of the ancient stones of prosperity and protection, Jade imbues the soul with serenity. It has traditionally been used to heal the kidneys and balance fluids in the body. Inspires dreams, stimulates ideas and instils self-sufficiency.

Chrysocolla (monoclinic/orthorhombic; blue-green) A tranquil crystal, Chrysocolla assists in both meditation and spiritual communication. It helps you to accept with serenity situations that cannot be changed and to keep silent when appropriate. It enhances self-awareness and confidence, promoting truthfulness and a cool head.

Turquoise (triclinic; blue-green) Highly prized since ancient times as an excellent healer and protector, Turquoise consoles the soul. Useful for problem-solving, it promotes self-realization and alleviates feelings of martyrdom or self-sabotage. Useful for strengthening the meridians and alleviating cramps and pain.

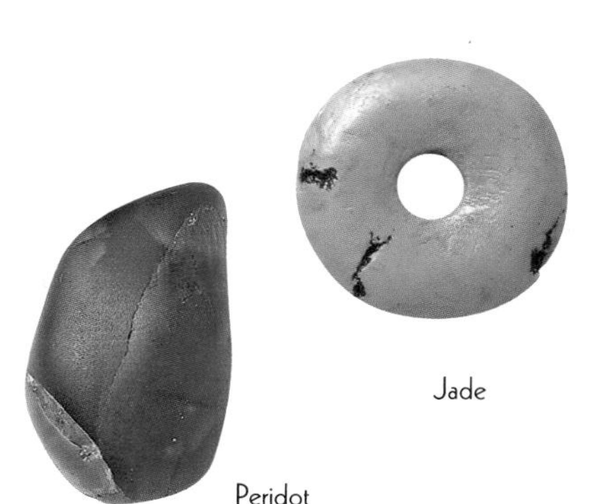

Jade

Peridot

Chrysocolla

Turquoise

Blue Lace Agate (trigonal; blue)
A great throat, thyroid and eye healer, Blue Lace Agate is calming and nurturing, bringing about inner peace. Transmuting anger, infection and inflammation, it helps you to express thoughts clearly and to stop suppressing feelings. All Agates enhance mental function, ameliorate confusion and overcome bitterness of the heart.

Kyanite (triclinic; blue, black)
The striations of tranquillizing Kyanite powerfully transmit and attract energy. Useful for dream-recall and transitions of any kind, Kyanite cleanses the meridians and energy lines and cuts through pretence. Dispels illusions and frustration and increases the capacity for logical, linear thought.

Lapis Lazuli (cubic; blue with gold)
Helpful for the throat and third eye, Lapis Lazuli heals problems associated with not speaking out. Harmonizing all the levels of being, it helps you to access your purpose in life. Lets you take charge of your life and brings deep self-knowledge.

Sugilite (hexagonal; purple)
One of the major love stones, Sugilite shows how to live your truth. Useful for healing dyslexia and trauma, it is particularly helpful for misfits. Sugilite helps you to overcome shock, upsets and disappointment. A useful crystal for groups, it dissipates hostility and instils forgiveness. Helps you to face up to and alleviate unpleasant emotional truths.

Kyanite
Lapis Lazuli
Blue Lace Agate
Sugilite

Amethyst (trigonal; purple) A highly protective crystal, Amethyst acts as a natural tranquillizer, balancing emotional highs and lows and counteracting geopathic stress. Useful for boosting hormones, it helps neural signals to pass through the brain. Facilitates decision-making and helps you free, less scattered and in setting realistic goals.

Fluorite (cubic; most colours) A useful viral healer, Fluorite is traditionally used to strengthen bones and teeth. Preventing dis-ease from electromagnetic stress, it dissolves fixed patterns. Fluorite helps you to discern when outside influences are affecting your behaviour. It also works to dissolve fixed ideas so that you see the bigger picture. Removes illusion and reveals truth.

Quartz (trigonal; white) One of the most energetic stones on the planet and a master healer, Quartz generates, conserves, amplifies or releases energy, as required. In its many forms, it works at the level appropriate to you. A natural storehouse of information, it assists concentration. Different varieties offer a wide spectrum of qualities.

Apophyllite (tetragonal; white) An excellent activator of intuition and spiritual vision, Apophyllite is a powerful vibrational transmitter. It promotes introspection and insight into causes of behaviour and any dis-ease you may have and is useful for Reiki. Alleviating apprehension, it allows you to tolerate uncertainty and make decisions from your spirit rather than your ego. Helps to overcome anxiety.

Purple Fluorite

Amethyst

Quartz

Apophyllite

Hematite (trigonal; red, silver when polished) One of the most useful grounding stones, Hematite harmonizes body, mind and spirit. Strongly yang, it balances the meridians, focuses concentration and supports when you feel vulnerable. Excellent for imparting confidence and also for enhancing willpower.

Smoky Quartz (trigonal; brown-grey) An excellent grounding and detoxifying crystal, Smoky Quartz is useful for protection especially against geopathic stress. It relieves depression and assists you in accepting your physical body, enhancing virility and potency. This crystal helps you to feel more comfortable in your body and in manifesting your dreams. Promotes positive, pragmatic thought.

Tourmaline (trigonal; most colours) An excellent crystal against psychic attack, Black Tourmaline also protects against geopathic stress or environmental unrest. Other colours offer a wide range of healing options, especially for overcoming emotional dysfunction. Helps you to find solutions to specific problems and assists you in understanding yourself and others.

Smoky Quartz

Hematite

Green Tourmaline

CHOOSING AND CLEANSING EXERCISES

The exercises on the following pages will help you get to know your crystals and their properties and qualities. You will also learn how to keep them at their sparkling, energetic best and how to open your crystal intuition. Remember to record your experiences in the spaces provided in each exercise.

What's in my collection?

This exercise helps you to work out exactly which crystals you have in your collection and what you can use them for. It also allows you to keep track of the additional discoveries you make as you explore your crystals in later activities in the book. Remember to date all entries.

Exercise 1 IDENTIFYING MY CRYSTALS

- **Using either the Crystal Directory** on pages 26–32 or *The Crystal Bible* volume 1 or volume 2, identify each crystal in your collection and list it in the fill-in spaces between pages 35 and 39.
- **Write down the crystal's known properties** and any effects you have noticed when holding or working with it. There is space to fill in new discoveries as you work through the book.
- **Date the entry** so that you can track your increasing knowledge and insight.
- **As you add new crystals to your collection,** be sure to list them and also list any different colours or forms of basic crystals, such as Jasper or Quartz.

My crystal collection

Crystal Amethyst

Date first worked with 2nd May Time 20-9am

Properties/effects

Additional discoveries

Date

Crystal Selenite

Date first worked with May 2nd Time 11:10

Properties/effects

Additional discoveries

Date

Crystal Citrine

Date first worked with May 1st Time 15:25, 20-9am

Properties/effects

Additional discoveries

Date

Crystal Black Tourmaline

Date first worked with Time

Properties/effects

Additional discoveries

Date

Crystal Calcite

Date first worked with May 2nd Time 15:52

Properties/effects

Additional discoveries

Date

Crystal Pink Aragonite

Date first worked with Time

Properties/effects

Additional discoveries

Date

Crystal Smokey Quartz

Date first worked with ______________ Time ______________

Properties/effects ______________

____

Additional discoveries ______________

____

______________ Date ______________

Crystal Carnelian

Date first worked with ______________ Time ______________

Properties/effects ______________

____

Additional discoveries ______________

____

______________ Date ______________

Crystal lapis lazuli

Date first worked with ______________ Time ______________

Properties/effects ______________

____

Additional discoveries ______________

____

______________ Date ______________

Crystal Clear Quartz

Date first worked with May 2nd Time 20- 9am

Properties/effects

Additional discoveries

Date

Crystal

Date first worked with Time

Properties/effects

Additional discoveries

Date

Crystal

Date first worked with Time

Properties/effects

Additional discoveries

Date

Crystal

Date first worked with Time

Properties/effects

Additional discoveries

Date

Crystal

Date first worked with Time

Properties/effects

Additional discoveries

Date

Crystal

Date first worked with Time

Properties/effects

Additional discoveries

Date

Using my intuition

This exercise helps you to become aware of which crystals are calling to you or would like to work with you. If you already dowse using a pendulum, use that method or, for a change, explore this finger-dowsing technique.

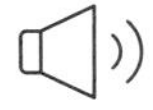

Exercise 2 WHAT DO MY FINGERS TELL ME?

AUDIO REFERENCE TRACK 3 (OPTIONAL)

- **You will need** a selection of crystals (already cleansed, see pages 22–23)
- **Placing your finger on one crystal** at a time ask, 'Is this the most appropriate and beneficial crystal to work with at this time?' If you have a specific goal, state what it is as you ask the question.
- **Loop one thumb and finger together** as shown on page 21, then loop the thumb and finger of the other hand through and pull. If the loop holds, the answer is yes. If the loop does not hold, select another crystal and repeat the process.
- **Make a record of the crystals** that responded positively to your question and your specific goal, if you had one.
- **To extend this exercise**, go into a crystal shop and finger dowse until you find the crystals that are beneficial for you once cleansed. You could also plunge your hand into a tub of tumbled crystal and see which ones 'stick' to your fingers. Now record your experiences in the space provided.

What my fingers told me

Crystal ______________________________

Date ______________________ Time ______________________

Goal ______________________________

____

Result ______________________________

____

Crystal ______________________________

Date ______________________ Time ______________________

Goal ______________________________

____

Result ______________________________

____

Crystal ______________________________

Date ______________________ Time ______________________

Goal ______________________________

____

Result ______________________________

____

Cleansing and activating

Carry out this exercise before using the crystals in your collection for the first time and repeat it whenever you add a new crystal or work on one of the exercises. It is especially important to cleanse your crystals after healing work.

Exercise 3 THE BIG CRYSTAL CLEANSE

- **You will need** crystals from your collection, a tub of uncooked brown rice, running water, a net bag, a cloth for drying
- **On a sunny day gather together** all your crystals. Sort them into two piles: robust tumbled, shaped or raw stones; and delicate layered crystals, clusters and those that may dissolve in water.
- **Place the delicate stones** in the tub of rice and leave for several hours (or overnight). As you do so, ask that the crystals be cleansed and purified.
- **If possible carry the more robust crystals** to a natural place where water runs freely or use spring water. Either place the crystals in the water directly or place them in the net bag first if there is a danger of them being washed away. As you do so, ask that the crystals be cleansed and purified.
- **Carefully dry the wet crystals** and place them in the sun for as long as possible to revitalize and recharge them (white stones like to be placed outside beneath the light of the moon, too). If possible, place the crystals directly onto the earth or a rock during this recharging period.
- **Hold the cleansed crystals in your hands**, or place your hands over the crystals if they are too large to hold. Picture them surrounded by bright white light and ask that the crystals work for your highest good and the highest good of anyone who has contact with them.

- **Wait a moment while the crystals adjust** to your unique resonance and come into harmony with your energy.
- **If you have a specific task for the crystals**, such as healing or protection, ask for that now, but do not limit your request; always add 'or something better', and/or 'anything else that the crystal wishes to offer me'.

My crystal cleanse experience

Date ______________________ **Time** ______________________

Crystals ______________________

My experience ______________________

____

Did I notice a difference in the crystals after they had been cleansed? ______________________

____

Did I notice a difference after they had been activated? ______________________

____

Did it become obvious that the crystal could help me in a specific way? ______________________

____

Crystal attunement

This exercise helps you to attune your own vibrations to those of a crystal so that you become more sensitive to crystal energies. You can use the audio track to get to know any crystal in your collection and experience its energy; just work with one cleansed and activated crystal (see pages 22–23) in turn. The audio talks you into a relaxed state, attunes you to the crystal, allows meditation time with the crystal, and then brings you out of the meditation. After each attunement, jot down any sensations you notice in your body, thoughts that come to mind or emotions you experience. Remember to add any new properties you discover to the crystal's entry on pages 34–39.

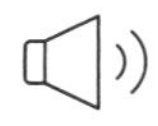

Exercise 4 ATTUNING TO MY CRYSTALS

AUDIO REFERENCE TRACK 2

TO FOLLOW THE SCRIPT TURN TO PAGES 244–245

- **You will need**: any cleansed and activated crystal from your collection
- **Sit quietly holding** your crystal. Breathe gently and allow yourself to relax and focus your attention on the crystal. State your intention to get to know this crystal a little better and to feel its energy.
- **Allow your eyes to go into soft focus** and gaze at the crystal. Note its shape, its colour and size. Follow its contours and craters, if it has a 'window' look inside. Feel how light or heavy the crystal is in your hand. Sense its vibrations and energetic resonance. You may feel your energy jump or tingle – like getting an electric shock – or slow and pulse as it connects to the crystal's energy. Allow the energy of the crystal to travel up your arms and into your heart and mind so that it reveals itself to you.

- **Notice whether the crystal makes a special contact** with any part of your body. If you wish, guide the energy up through your chakras (see pages 82–83) and watch for an energetic response.
- **If the crystal is transparent or translucent**, allow your gaze to pass through the outer edge and into the centre; follow the planes and landscape you find there. Crystal energy is subtle, so allow yourself time to attune to the vibrations.
- **When you are ready, put your crystal down** and consciously break contact with its energies. Open your eyes fully and bring your attention into the room. Take your focus to your feet and feel the contact they make with the floor. Feel the contact your sit bones make with the chair; feel them supporting the weight of your body. Picture a bubble of protection all around you. When you feel ready, stand up and move around, then record your insights in the space provided.

Note: Try using both your left and right hands separately to feel the energy as one hand may be more receptive then the other. If so, use this hand in future exercises.

My crystal attunement experience

Crystal ______________________________

Date ____________________ **Time** ____________________

My experience ______________________________

____

____

My body sensations ______________________________

____

My receptive hand ______________________________

My chakra connections ______________________________

____

____

My thoughts ______________________________

____

____

My emotions ______________________________

____

____

My intuitive understanding of what the crystal is offering me ______________________________

____

____

My crystal attunement experience

Crystal ____

Date ______________________ **Time** ______________________

My experience ____

____

____

My body sensations ____

____

____

My chakra connections ____

____

____

My thoughts ____

____

____

My emotions ____

____

____

My intuitive understanding of what the crystal is offering me ______________

____

____

My crystal attunement experience

Crystal ____________________

Date ____________________ **Time** ____________________

My experience ____________________

____

____

My body sensations ____________________

____

____

My chakra connections ____________________

____

____

My thoughts ____________________

____

____

My emotions ____________________

____

____

My intuitive understanding of what the crystal is offering me ____________________

____

____

ALL ABOUT CRYSTALS

What is a crystal?

Most people think of sparkling gemstones when they hear the word 'crystal', but strictly speaking, a crystal is defined as having an orderly, identifiable repeating lattice or internal structure. For the purposes of crystal healing, all kinds of stones – including Flint, meteorites and solidified resins such as Amber – are referred to as crystals, regardless of whether they are gemstones, semi-precious stones, pieces of rock or amorphous substances.

How do crystals work?

The blunt answer to this question is that no one knows exactly! People talk about colour resonances between crystals and the chakras (see pages 88–89), about the effects of light and energy on our bodies and the fact that our bodies contain a huge volume of water through which vibrations can pass. But quite why they work as they do is something that we may have to leave to quantum science to explain – which suggests that waves and particles are the same and can be in two places at once. What we do know, however, is that although they may look calm on the outside, internally crystals form a seething mass of energy as their tiny particles vibrate around atomic cores. Whatever else crystals do, they most certainly emit and absorb energies, and this energy can be measured – and experienced.

Ancient peoples believed that everything on and in the earth and the sky was a manifestation of the divine and that crystals were the flesh of the gods. As such, they could be used to attract the benevolent attentions – or deflect the malevolent intentions – of the gods. People believed in the concept of 'as above, so below' and of correspondences and similarities. This theory suggests that there is a resonating order throughout the universe and that any part can be used to bring about harmony in the whole, especially where there is a resemblance between the two parts.

Although it arrived on the planet from outer space and does not have a crystalline structure, Moldavite is nevertheless deemed to be a crystal.

Magnesite's similarity to bone caused ancient people to use it for skeletal healing and tooth problems.

Zincite's resemblance to urine crystals prompted a modern crystal healer to suggest its use for urinary infections.

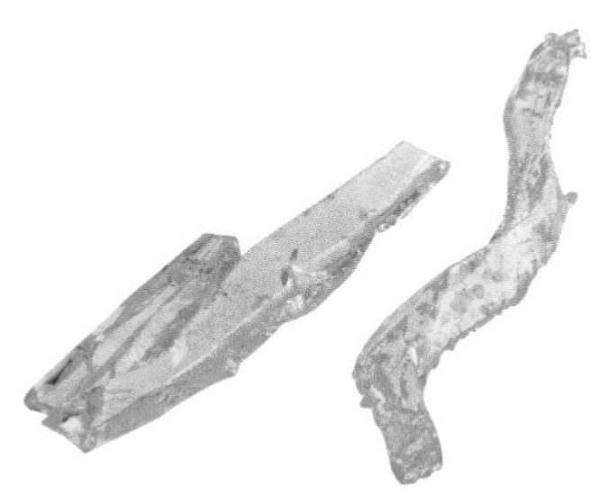

This exercise is suitable for Any crystal or rock.

Work with your crystals now To experience the energies of very different crystals, turn to Exercise 5: Feel Me on page 66.

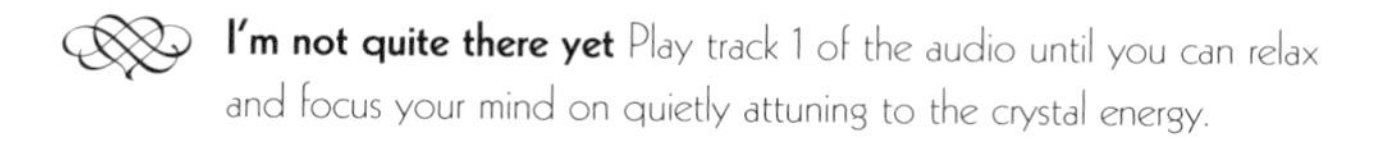

I'm not quite there yet Play track 1 of the audio until you can relax and focus your mind on quietly attuning to the crystal energy.

Do shape and colour matter?

Indeed they do! Both the colour and the shape of a crystal can affect how its energy flows and the healing work it can do, and attuning yourself to specific colours and shapes expands your knowledge of the ways in which crystals want to work with you. Both colour and shape can be artificially amended, which affects how the underlying energies manifest.

Crystal colours

Within their main form, many crystals can be found in a variety of colours. Colour arises from the minerals and impurities incorporated when the crystal is created or superheated, although some are artificially dyed or heat-amended to produce a different colour – for example Amethyst or Smoky Quartz are heated to form Citrine or Prasiolite, and Mohave Turquoise is dyed deep purple. As a general guide, the following colours have specific effects or properties. However, do not let this limit what an individual crystal can do for you.

Crystal shapes

The internal lattice of a crystal defines the system to which it belongs and affects how energy moves through the crystal. This internal lattice and its precise replication of facets and angles remains the same no matter how the crystal is shaped on the outside – which is why a crystal can be raw or faceted,

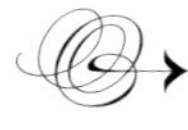

These exercises are suitable for All colours and shapes of crystal.

Work with your crystals now Select the crystal colours or shapes you wish to experience and then turn to Exercise 6: Which Colour Am I? on page 70 or Exercise 3: What Shape Am I? on page 74.

I'm not quite there yet Study the crystal shapes in your collection and compare them with those on pages 58–61 so that you can quickly identify the different forms.

flawless or chipped and still have the same healing effect. A few crystals that formed rapidly, such as Obsidian, and the resin Amber do not have an internal lattice (see pages 63–64). Regardless of the structure of the internal lattice, the flow of crystal energy is also mediated by the way in which a crystal is shaped externally, whether naturally or by cutting and polishing (see pages 58–61). If you are a beginner, it is easier to start experiencing energy flow by working with shaped crystals before moving on to use the more subtle internal lattice of crystal systems (see pages 63–64).

Crystal variations

Although these stones below and on page 55 all look very different, they are all classified as crystals by crystal enthusiasts. Some crystals are artificially shaped to look different and for specific purposes.

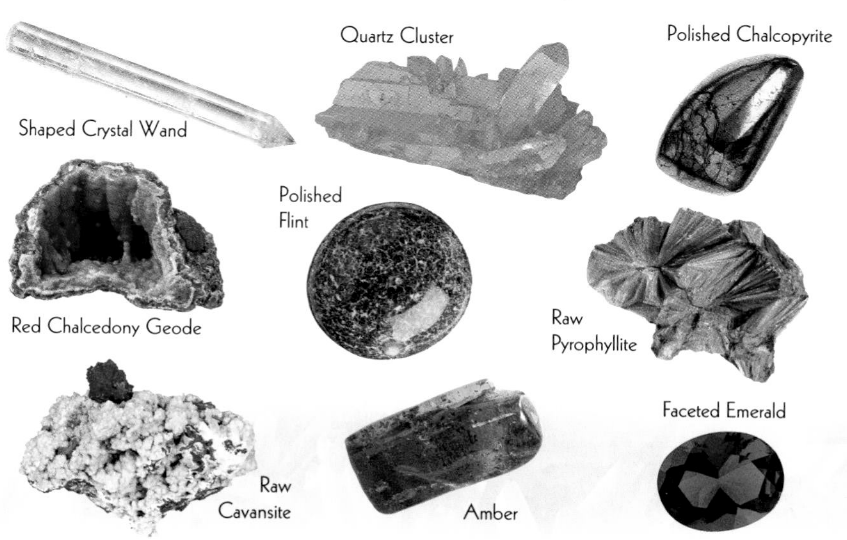

Crystalline Hemimorphite

Polished Preseli Bluestone

Natural Pumice

Polished Rhodocrosite

Polished Malachite

Tumbled Lapis Lazuli

Raw Amazonite

Natural Spirit Quartz

Raw Yellow Calcite

Polished Fluorite

DIRECTORY OF COLOURS

Rose Quartz

Pink crystals Offering unconditional love, nurturing and comfort, these crystals are excellent for healing the heart, releasing grief, calming emotions and instilling acceptance. Ideal for long-term use.

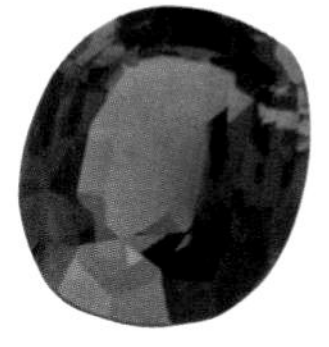

Faceted Ruby

Red crystals Stimulating and strengthening, these crystals are superb for activating creativity and revitalizing potency, but may over-excite volatile emotions. They are traditionally used for alleviating haemorrhages and inflammation. Best for short-term use.

Carnelian

Orange crystals Activating and releasing, these crystals are useful for building up energetic structures. Many attract abundance and stimulate creativity.

Yellow crystals Awakening and organizing, these crystals are particularly active at the mental level and the solar plexus. They calm the emotions and infections. Useful for overcoming seasonal disorders.

Citrine

Green crystals Calming and balancing, these crystals provide healing for the eyes and heart. They are useful when energy needs sedating or emotions need pacifying. Traditionally used for diseases of the eye.

Malachite

Blue crystals Calming and facilitating clear communication and self-expression. These crystals can ground or project spiritual energy. Assist intuition and channeling.

Angelite

Fluorite

Purple, indigo and lilac crystals Integrating and aligning, these crystals have powerful spiritual-awakening qualities, stimulating service to others. Useful for cooling over-heated energies.

Snow Quartz

White or clear crystals Purifing and focusing energy, these crystals link to the highest realms of being. Excellent when situations need clarifying or for opening intuition and gaining insight.

Tiger's Eye

Grey, brown or black crystals Good for grounding the physical body and detoxifying negative energies, these crystals are useful protectors. Helpful in grids.

DIRECTORY OF SHAPES

Ball Emits energy equally all round. Forms a window to move through time.

Quartz ball

Cluster Several points on a base radiate energy in several directions.

Quartz cluster

Double terminated Points at both ends emit energy. Breaks old patterns.

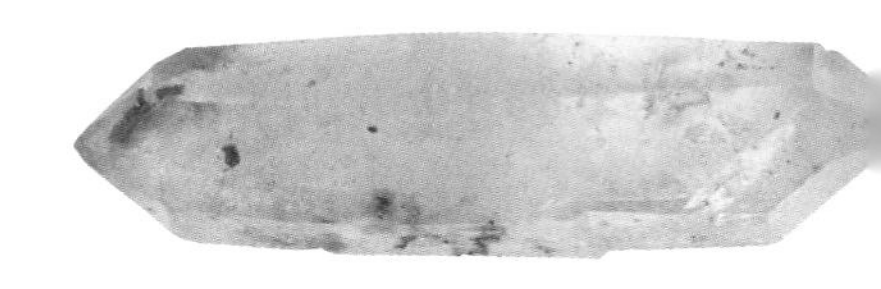

Double-terminated Quartz wand

Zoisite egg

Egg The gently pointed end focuses energy.

Elestial

Elestial Gently folded crystal with many terminations, windows and inner planes. Radiates a gently flowing energy that opens the way to insight and change.

Quartz generator point

Generator Features a six-pointed end or several points radiating equally in all directions. Focuses healing energy or intention and draws people together.

Geode Hollow cave-like formation that amplifies, conserves and slowly releases energy.

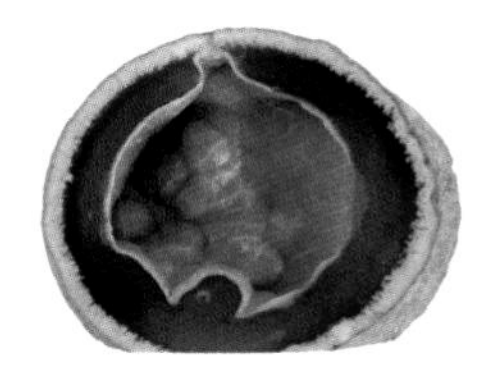

Avalonite geode

Phantom Features a pointed inner pyramid. Breaks old patterns and raises vibrations.

Quartz phantom

Point Draws off energy when pointed out from the body, draws energy in when pointed toward the body. Useful for cleansing and energizing.

Amethyst point

Square Consolidates energy and useful for anchoring intention and grounding. Naturally occurring square crystals, such as Fluorite, draw off negative energy and transform it.

Natural Fluorite square

Quartz sceptre

Sceptre Crystal formed around a central core rod. An excellent power and restructuring tool.

Tumbled Amphibole

Tumbled Gently rounded stones. Useful in grids or to wear to draw off negative energy or bring in positive vibrations.

Twin

Twin Two crystals of equal length sharing a base. Draws people together.

Natural Quartz wand

Wand Long pointed or specially shaped crystals. Either focus and draw off energy or bring in energy according to which way the point is facing. Useful for joining crystals in a grid.

Crystal systems

Geologists and gemologists assign crystals to seven main groups according to their inner geometric lattice: cubic, hexagonal, monoclinic, orthorhombic, tetragonal, triclinic and trigonal. There is one further category of crystal, amorphous, which has no lattice because of the speed at which it formed. Each of these groups of crystal is built from a basic shape, but this does not necessarily affect the outer appearance of the crystal. Crystals from these groups are used in advanced healing techniques.

This exercise is suitable for Crystals from each of the eight systems.

Work with your crystals now To explore crystal systems, turn to Exercise 8: What System Do I Belong To? on page 78.

Note This exercise is for advanced practitioners who can identify the system to which a crystal belongs and understand energy utilization.

I'm not quite there yet If you don't know to which system your crystal belongs, check in the Crystal Directory on pages 26–32 or in other reference books. If you don't feel ready for advanced work, spend more time exploring how energy moves through external crystal shapes (see pages 58–61), or turn to the next chapter on page 81 or move onto the other exercises.

DIRECTORY OF GROUPS

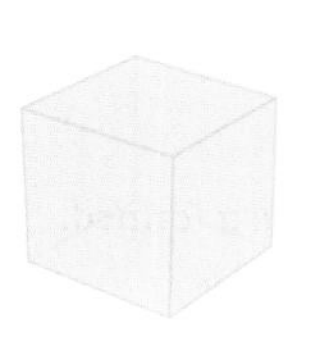

Almandine Garnet

Cubic (lattice created from squares with axes at right angles to each other; e.g. Garnet) Stabilizes, grounds, cleanses, releases tension and encourages creativity.

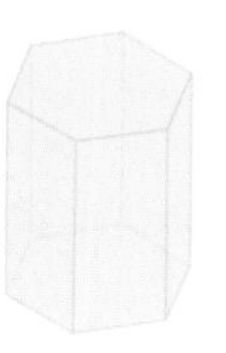

Faceted Emerald

Hexagonal (lattice created from three-dimensional hexagrams; e.g. Emerald) Organizes and balances energy and provides support; useful for exploring specific issues.

Polished Selenite

Monoclinic (lattice created from parallelograms; e.g. Selenite) Increases perception and balances the body systems; excellent for purification.

Danburite

Orthorhombic (lattice created from rhomboids; e.g. Danburite) Useful cleanser and clearer; increases the flow of information.

Tetragonal (lattice created from rectangles with long and short axes at right angles to each other; e.g. Apophyllite) Transforms, opens, harmonizes and balances energy flow; brings resolution.

Natural Apophyllite pyramid

Triclinic (lattice formed from trapeziums; e.g. Labradorite) Protects and opens perception, facilitating exploration of other dimensions.

Labradorite

Trigonal (lattice created from triangles; e.g. Tourmaline) Focuses and anchors energy; invigorates and protects the aura.

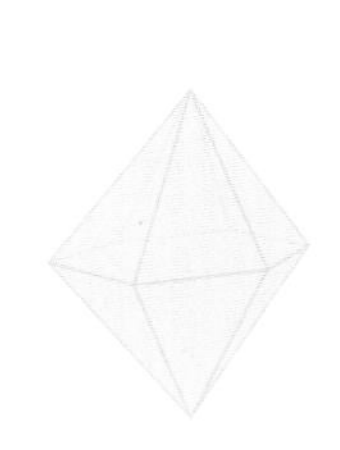

Tourmaline

Amorphous (no lattice; e.g. Obsidian) Energy flows and acts rapidly; can be a catalyst for growth or catharsis.

Obsidian

SHAPE AND COLOUR EXERCISES

The following exercises will help you to understand crystal energies and shapes and to intuitively feel the effect they have on you and your environment. Crystal energies are subtle and may not be experienced in quite the way you expect. Watch out for sensations, either on the surface of your skin or deep within your body, or for feelings out in the aura or around your head or feet. Crystals have their own way of communicating with you, so just relax, be patient and wait for them to make their energy known. The more you can become one with the crystal, the more conscious you will be of the energy to which you are attuning.

Feeling crystal energies

Some people are immediately aware of crystal energies, describing them as 'buzzing', 'jumping' or 'stimulating', or 'soothing' and 'a stream of energy'. Other people find that their moods or mind are more subtly affected. But by practising this exercise, anyone can learn to sense crystal energies in one way or another and to differentiate between the different shapes.

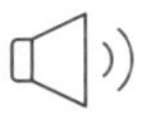

Exercise 5 FEEL ME

AUDIO REFERENCE TRACK 2 (TO FOLLOW THE SCRIPT, TURN TO PAGES 244–45)

- **You will need** 4 or 5 cleansed and activated crystals or stones of various shapes and/or colours, such as a piece of Flint, some Amber, a gemstone, a rough semi-precious crystal, such as Lapis Lazuli, and a piece of Quartz
- **Relax and place your hand** over each of the crystals in turn and wait to see if you can feel its energy. If you can, record your findings in the spaces provided. If you can't yet sense the energy, play Track 2 of the audio, or change hands.
- **As you follow the instructions** on the audio and allow yourself to relax, open your mind's eye and focus your attention gently on the crystal you are holding. Feel its shape and weight and become one with the crystal and the energies it is resonating. Does it feel fast or slow, hot or cold?
- **When you have experienced the energy** of one crystal, pick up another very different type and repeat the process, noticing the differences.
- **Finally, put all the crystals down** on a table, mix them around and, with your eyes closed, try to identify which crystal is which from its energetic feel. Now record your experiences in the space provided.

My crystal energy experience

Date ______________________ **Time** ______________________

Crystal 1 ______________________

Shape ______________________ **Colour** ______________________

How did the crystal energy feel? ______________________

How did it affect me? ______________________

Did it affect a specific part of my body? ______________________

Did it change my mood? ______________________

Did it bring up a particular emotion or thought? ______________________

Crystal 2 ______________________________

Shape ____________________ **Colour** ____________________

How did the crystal energy feel? ______________________________

____

How did it affect me? ______________________________

____

Did it affect a specific part of my body? ______________________________

Did it change my mood? ______________________________

Did it bring up a particular emotion or thought? ______________________________

How was it different from the first crystal? ______________________________

Crystal 3 ______________________________

Shape ____________________ **Colour** ____________________

How did the crystal energy feel? ______________________________

____

How did it affect me? ______________________________

____

Did it affect a specific part of my body? ______________________________

Did it change my mood? ______________________________

Did it bring up a particular emotion or thought? ______________________________

How was it different from the other crystals? ______________________________

Crystal 4 ______________________________

Shape ______________ **Colour** ______________

How did the crystal energy feel? ______________________________

____

How did it affect me? ______________________________

____

Did it affect a specific part of my body? ______________________________

Did it change my mood? ______________________________

Did it bring up a particular emotion or thought? ______________________________

How was it different from the first crystal? ______________________________

Crystal 5 ______________________________

Shape ______________ **Colour** ______________

How did the crystal energy feel? ______________________________

____

How did it affect me? ______________________________

____

Did it affect a specific part of my body? ______________________________

Did it change my mood? ______________________________

Did it bring up a particular emotion or thought? ______________________________

How was it different from the other crystals? ______________________________

Experiencing colour

This exercise helps you to understand the effect colour brings to a specific crystal and to identify which ones work best for you. You can also use this exercise to work with different colours of crystal generally rather than comparing those of one type only. Remember to use your receptive hand.

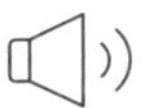

Exercise 6 WHICH COLOUR AM I?

AUDIO REFERENCE TRACK 3 (OPTIONAL)

- **You will need** a cleansed and activated crystals, such as Jasper or Quartz, in as many different colours as possible, a table, a white cloth
- **Pick one colour of the crystal** and hold it quietly for a few moments. Notice whether it feels hot or cold, lively or calming, and any immediate effect it has on you at the physical, emotional, mental, auric or spiritual level. Particularly note if you are especially attracted or repulsed by the crystal (you can work with this later, see pages 118–19).
- **Hold the crystal at a distance** from your body, then bring it close to you and see how it feels. Does its energy get stronger? Does your body respond? Does your mood or thought-pattern change?
- **Beginning at the top of your head,** slowly pass the crystal down the mid-line of your body and notice any sensations you feel.

- **Stop at each chakra (see pages 82–83)** and check the effect, if any, that a particular colour of crystal has on that chakra.
- **Repeat with another colour**. When you have worked with each of the colours, put all the crystals on a table on a neutral base, such as a white cloth. Close your eyes and swirl the crystals around several times.
- **Keeping your eyes closed**, pick up each crystal in turn and try to name the colour. Write down your thoughts in the space provided.
- **Repeat the exercise at a different** time of day and practise until you can correctly identify each colour. Don't forget to record and date your observations.

My crystal colour experience

Crystal ______________________________

Date ______________ **Time** ______________

My experience with red ______________________________

My experience with orange ______________________________

My experience with yellow ______________________________

My experience with blue ______________________________

My experience with green ______________________________

My experience with brown ______________________________

My experience with silver ______________________________

My experience with gold ______________________________

My experience with multi-coloured stones ______________________________

How did the different colours vary in their effect? ______________________________

Which chakras or parts of my body were affected? ______________________________

Did they affect my mood or mental pattern? ______________________________

Was I able to distinguish one colour from another with my eyes closed? ______________________________

Experiencing shape

Now that you are beginning to easily experience how crystal energy feels and moves, it is time to move on and experience its effects on and around you and in your environment.

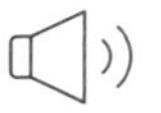

Exercise 7 WHICH SHAPE AM I?

AUDIO REFERENCE TRACK 2 OR 3 (OPTIONAL)

- **You will need:** a cleansed and activated crystal ball, 7 crystal points, crystal wand or long point, tumbled crystal, geode, cluster and other crystal shapes
- **Taking each shape in turn**, hold it in your hands and attune to it. Allow yourself to feel how energy circulates in the vicinity of the crystal. Ask yourself if energy is drawn toward the crystal or given out from it.
- **Move the crystal toward and then away** from your body, and try to be aware of the effect that the shape has. Does it pull energy away from you or toward you? Does it feel comforting or disturbing?
- **Now put the crystal somewhere** in your environment, perhaps on your bedside table. If the crystal has a point, become aware of the difference in energy if the point is facing toward or away from you. Tune into how you feel about the crystal shape being there. Turn it in different directions until it feels comfortable for you. If it feels appropriate, sleep with the crystal in position overnight and see if it makes a difference to how you sleep and what you dream about. Remember to make a record of the results.
- **Now take the seven crystal points** and lie down with them spaced equally around your head, points facing outward. Give yourself five minutes or so to feel how the energy affects you. Then turn the stones point in and again give yourself five minutes or so to experience the energy.

- **Holding the crystal wand** with the point facing away from you, spiral out from each of your chakras in turn (see page 84). Then turn the crystal point inward (cleansing it first, if appropriate) and spiral back into each chakra (spiral out in whichever direction feels good to you and then back in the opposite direction).

Try the same exercises using the same shapes in a different type of crystal and see how this changes the energy or the feelings you are aware of. Now record your experience in the space provided.

My crystal shape experience

Crystal ______________________ **Shape** ______________________

Date ______________________ **Time** ______________________

When I held the crystal shape it felt ______________________

The energy was drawn (in or out) ______________________

When I brought the crystal toward myself I felt ______________________

When I moved the crystal away from myself I felt ______________________

When the crystal was in my environment it felt ______________________

When I turned the crystal around it ______________________

It affected my sleep and my dreams in this way ______________________

____

Did it assist/not assist my dream recall? ______________________

When I changed the shape of crystal I experienced ______________________

Crystal ______________________ **Shape** ______________________

Date ______________________ **Time** ______________________

When I held the crystal shape it felt ______________________

The energy was drawn (in or out) ______________________

When I brought the crystal toward myself I felt ______________________

When I moved the crystal away from myself I felt ______________________

When the crystal was in my environment it felt ______________________

When I turned the crystal around it ______________________

It affected my sleep and my dreams in this way ______________________

Did it assist/not assist my dream recall? ______________________

When I changed the shape of crystal I experienced ______________________

Crystal ______________________ **Shape** ______________________

Date ______________________ **Time** ______________________

When I held the crystal shape it felt ______________________

The energy was drawn (in or out) ______________________

When I brought the crystal shape toward myself I felt ______________________

When I moved the crystal shape away from myself I felt ______________________

When the crystal shape was in my environment it felt ______________________

When I turned the crystal around it ______________________

It affected my sleep and my dreams in this way ______________________

Did it assist/not assist my dream recall? ______________________

When I changed the type of crystal I experienced ______________________

Crystal ______________________ **Shape** ______________________

Date ______________________ **Time** ______________________

When I held the crystal points it felt ______________________

The energy was drawn (in or out) ______________________

When I placed the points towards my head it felt ______________________

____

When I placed the points outward from my head it felt ______________________

When I changed the type of crystal I experienced ______________________

____

Crystal ______________________ **Shape** ______________________

Date ______________________ **Time** ______________________

When I held the crystal shape it felt ______________________

____

The energy was drawn (in or out) ______________________

____

When I brought the crystal toward myself I felt ______________________

____

When I moved the crystal away from myself I felt ______________________

____

When I spiralled the wand out from my chakras it ______________________

____

When I spiralled the wand in toward my chakras it ______________________

____

Exploring crystal systems

Because crystal systems are more subtle than colour or form, it can take time to become aware of the effect of their energies, and it is not essential to remember the systems, so this is an exercise to return to as you become more sensitized to crystals. These systems are used in advanced crystal healing, but you can sample their energies by placing the crystals on your solar plexus. Do first check that you have grasped the basic building blocks of the crystal systems by completing the identification exercise below.

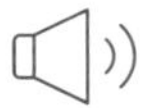

Exercise 8 WHAT SYSTEM DO I BELONG TO?

AUDIO REFERENCE TRACK 3 (OPTIONAL)

- **You will need**: a cleansed and activated crystal from each of the eight groups (see pages 63–64 and the Crystal Directory on pages 26–32)
- **Lie down and place a crystal** from the first group on your solar plexus for about five minutes. Notice where in your body, mind, emotions, spirit or chakras you can feel the effect.
- **Think about whether you are aware** of energy moving from, through or into the crystal.
- **Record your results** and then repeat the exercise with the next example of a crystal system. Repeat until you have experienced a crystal from each of the eight groups. If you don't resonate with one crystal, try another.

My crystal system experience

Crystal ______________________________ **System** cubic

Date ______________ **Time** ______________

My thoughts on the effect of this crystal system ______________

Energy moved in this direction ______________

Crystal ______________________________ **System** hexagonal

Date ______________ **Time** ______________

My thoughts on the effect of this crystal system ______________

Energy moved in this direction ______________

Crystal ______________________________ **System** monoclinic

Date ______________ **Time** ______________

My thoughts on the effect of this crystal system ______________

Energy moved in this direction ______________

Crystal ______________________________ **System** orthorhombic

Date ______________ **Time** ______________

My thoughts on the effect of this crystal system ______________

Energy moved in this direction ______________

Crystal ______________________ **System** tetragonal

Date ____________ **Time** ____________

My thoughts on the effect of this crystal system ______________________

Energy moved in this direction ______________________

Crystal ______________________ **System** triclinic

Date ____________ **Time** ____________

My thoughts on the effect of this crystal system ______________________

Energy moved in this direction ______________________

Crystal ______________________ **System** trigonal

Date ____________ **Time** ____________

My thoughts on the effect of this crystal system ______________________

Energy moved in this direction ______________________

Crystal ______________________ **System** amorphous

Date ____________ **Time** ____________

My thoughts on the effect of this crystal system ______________________

Energy moved in this direction ______________________

CRYSTALS AND THE CHAKRAS

Chakras and healing

Chakras are centres of energy in the body that distribute our life-force. They connect the physical body with the subtle bodies of the aura around it and with different spiritual dimensions. Traditionally, there are seven major chakras, but more are being re-discovered (see pages 92–96). Each one correlates with a specific crystal and colour (although many colours have been assigned to the chakras).

The different chakras govern different aspects of human emotion and behaviour, and how well each one is functioning determines whether that aspect of your being is in a state of harmony or disharmony. If a chakra becomes blocked, for example, your flow of subtle energy becomes imbalanced and dis-ease or disharmony on the physical, emotional, mental or spiritual level eventually results. This makes balancing the chakras an essential base for holistic healing.

To an intuitive eye chakras spin, looking like whirling wheels of light, although, despite what you might read, there is no one 'correct' direction of spin. Dull or black patches or a spin that 'wobbles' or is too fast or slow signify dis-ease at the physical, emotional, mental or spiritual level, according to the chakra concerned. Fortunately, you do not need to 'see' such dis-ease because a crystal picks up any disharmony, rectifies it and re-energizes the chakra.

By placing an appropriate crystal on a chakra, you can ameliorate any negative qualities or specific issues aligned with that chakra or support its positive properties (to find out which positive and negative qualities are associated with the chakras, see the charts on pages 84–87). If you have emotional, mental or spiritual issues connected to a specific chakra, your overall health will benefit if you place an appropriate crystal on the chakra and leave it there for 20 minutes or so while you relax (you might like to play the music-only track of the audio during your relaxation).

This exercise is suitable for Any crystal that your intuition or a reference book tells you is appropriate for your chakras, but especially Smoky Quartz, Red Jasper, Orange Carnelian, Yellow Jasper, Green Aventurine, Blue Lace Agate, Sodalite and Amethyst.

Work with your crystals now To cleanse and recharge your chakras, turn to Exercise 9: Full Chakra Cleanse, balance and recharge on pages 98–99.

I'm not quite there yet Study the chakra charts and diagrams on pages 84–87 until you fully understand the relationship between the chakras and the emotional or mental blocks that can create dis-ease.

THE POSITION OF THE CHAKRAS

1 **Earth chakra** Below feet, grounds into incarnation. Crystal: Smoky Quartz

2 **Base chakra** At the perineum; sexual and creative centre. Crystal: Red Jasper

3 **Sacral chakra** Just below the navel; the other sexual and creative centre. Crystal: Orange Carnelian

4 **Solar plexus chakra** At the solar plexus; emotional centre. Crystal: Yellow Jasper

5 **Heart seed chakra** At the base of the breastbone; site of soul remembrance (see also page 95). Crystal: Danburite

6 **Spleen chakra** Under left armpit; potential site of energy leakage. Crystal: Green Aventurine

7 **Heart chakra** Over the physical heart; love centre. Crystal: Rose Quartz

8 **Higher heart chakra** (see page 95) Crystal: Dioptase

9 **Throat chakra** Over the throat; centre of truth. Crystal: Blue Lace Agate

10 **Past-life** or **alta-major chakra** Just behind the ears; stores past-life information. Crystal: Variscite

11 **Third eye chakra** Midway between eyebrow and hairline; centre of insight. Crystal: Apophyllite

12 **Soma chakra** (see page 95) Crystal: Preseli Bluestone

13 **Crown chakra** At the top of the head; spiritual connection point. Crystal: Amethyst

14 **Soul star** (see page 96) Crystal: Pelalite

15 **Stellar gateway** (see page 96) Crystal: Azeztulite

Note: see also pages 92–96 for the higher vibrational chakras.

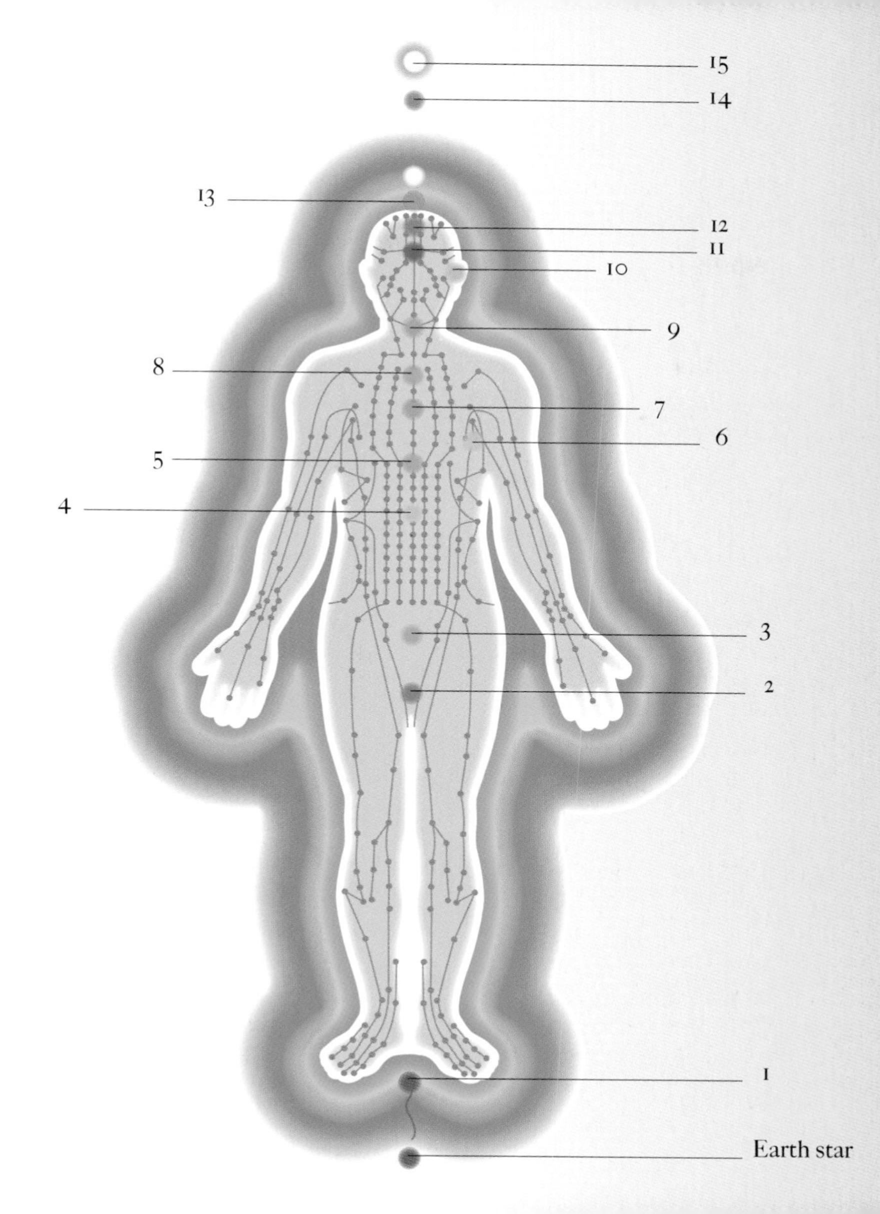
15
14
13
12
11
10
9
8
7
6
5
4
3
2
1
Earth star

CHAKRAS AND THEIR QUALITIES

Earth

COLOUR: Brown
POSITION: Below feet
ISSUE: Material connection and grounding
POSITIVE QUALITIES: grounded, practical, operates well in everyday reality
NEGATIVE QUALITIES: no sense of power or potency, cannot operate in everyday reality, picks up negativity

---

Base

COLOUR: Red
POSITION: Base of spine
ISSUE: Survival instincts
POSITIVE QUALITIES: Base security, sense of one's own power, active, independent, spontaneous leadership
NEGATIVE QUALITIES: Impatience, fear of annihilation, death wish, over-sexed or impotent, vengeful, violent, angry, hyperactive, impulsive, manipulative

---

Sacral

COLOUR: Orange
POSITION: Below navel
ISSUE: Creativity and procreation
POSITIVE QUALITIES: Fertility, courage, assertiveness, confidence, joy, sexuality, sensual pleasure, acceptance of sexual identity
NEGATIVE QUALITIES: Low self-esteem, infertility, cruelty, inferiority, sluggishness, pomposity, emotional hooks or thought forms

---

Solar plexus

COLOUR: Yellow
POSITION: Above navel
ISSUE: Emotional connection and assimilation
POSITIVE QUALITIES: Good energy utilization, empathetic, organized, logical, actively intelligent
NEGATIVE QUALITIES: Poor energy utilization, lazy, overly emotional or cold, cynical, has emotional baggage, leaches energy, takes on other people's feelings and problems

---

Spleen

COLOUR: Light green
POSITION: Under left arm
ISSUE: Energy leaching
POSITIVE QUALITIES: Self-contained, powerful
NEGATIVE QUALITIES: Exhausted and manipulated

Heart

COLOUR: Green
POSITION: Over heart
ISSUE: Love
POSITIVE QUALITIES: Loving, generous, compassionate, nurturing, flexible, self-confident, accepting
NEGATIVE QUALITIES: Disconnected from feelings, unable to show love, jealous, possessive, insecure, miserly or resistant to change

---

Throat

COLOUR: Blue
POSITION: Throat
ISSUE: Communication
POSITIVE QUALITIES: Able to speak own truth, receptive, idealistic, loyal
NEGATIVE QUALITIES: Incapable of verbalizing thoughts or feelings, stuck, dogmatic, disloyal

---

Third eye

COLOUR: Dark blue
POSITION: Forehead
ISSUE: Intuition and mental connection
POSITIVE QUALITIES: Intuitive, perceptive, visionary, in-the-moment
NEGATIVE QUALITIES: Spaced-out, fearful, attached to past, superstitious, bombarded with other people's thoughts

---

Past life

COLOUR: Light turquoise-green
POSITION: Behind ears
ISSUE: Anything carried over from past lives
POSITIVE QUALITIES: Wise, has life skills, instinctively knowing
NEGATIVE QUALITIES: Carries emotional baggage, insecure, has unfinished business

---

Crown

COLOUR: Violet
POSITION: Top of head
ISSUE: Spiritual connection
POSITIVE QUALITIES: Mystical, creative, humanitarian, giving service
NEGATIVE QUALITIES: Overly-imaginative, illusory, arrogant, exercises power to control others

Chakras and colour

Although in modern times chakras have been allocated specific colours based on the colours of the rainbow, the tradition of using crystals on the chakras dates from before these colours were allotted. On very early chakra diagrams, the chakras are shown in various colours, and there were often more than the 'traditional' seven chakras.

So when you are working with your crystals, you can either choose to use the modern colour correspondences (see right) or to find your own intuitive crystal correspondences. Knowing what alternatives there are is helpful if you want to sedate an overactive chakra. For instance, placing a red crystal on a base chakra that is spinning at full tilt and brimming with lust may only inflame the situation, whereas another colour could calm it (although paradoxically Red Jasper often calms this chakra when it is inflamed, so always check the effects for yourself).

Modern chakra colour correspondences

Earth Brown
Base chakra Red
Sacral chakra Orange
Solar plexus chakra Yellow
Heart chakra Green
Throat chakra Blue
Third eye chakra Indigo
Crown chakra Purple or white.

This exercise is suitable for Different-coloured crystals associated with the chakras (see above and pages 85–87)

Work with your crystals now To discover your own colour and chakra correspondences, turn to Exercise 10: What Colour Are My Chakras? on pages 102–3.

I'm not quite there yet Return to pages 55–57 to sensitize yourself more fully to crystal colours.

Chakras and the aura

If you have an intuitive eye, you may see an aura as a field of coloured lights around the physical body. This vital and energetic energy field is active, vibrating with interweaving layers and multi-coloured bands that relate to your physical, emotional, mental and spiritual states. It is linked to your physical body through the chakras, and if your chakras are balanced and in good order, they strengthen your aura and help to prevent energy 'leakage'.

The aura delineates 'your space'. If someone enters your inner auric field, you feel invaded, but energies, thoughts and feelings can penetrate the aura, even from a distance – and many auras extend into subtle multi-dimensional fields.

When negative energy, thoughts or feelings lodge in your aura they cause dis-ease, so cleansing your aura regularly is essential if you are to stay protected and energized. Crystals can also be used to heal 'holes' in the aura that arise from causes such as physical scarring or depletion by illness, emotional or mental pain. By strengthening the aura in this way, you make it impossible for other people to penetrate your personal space or leach your energy.

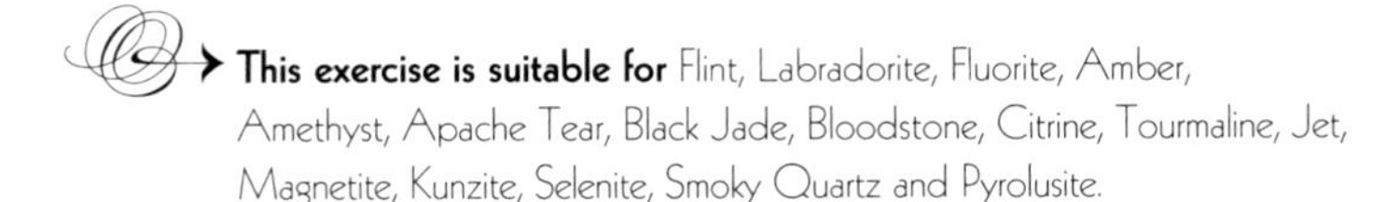

This exercise is suitable for Flint, Labradorite, Fluorite, Amber, Amethyst, Apache Tear, Black Jade, Bloodstone, Citrine, Tourmaline, Jet, Magnetite, Kunzite, Selenite, Smoky Quartz and Pyrolusite.

Work with your crystals now To cleanse, strengthen and repair your aura, turn to Exercise 11: Strengthening My Aura on page 104–5.

I'm not quite there yet Revise the method for selecting a crystal intuitively on pages 20–21, asking which crystals would be best for you to use for your aura.

Opening the higher chakras

As we move from the astrological age of Pisces to the age of Aquarius, changes in human consciousness are occurring. New dimensions are opening up, and additional chakras are becoming available to mediate the changing energy and to convert pure consciousness and higher dimensional vibrations into a form that can be assimilated by our earth bodies.

Our physical bodies access these vibrations through the lightbody, one of the subtle bodies held in the aura, and we link with the lightbody through the higher vibration chakras (see the illustration and chart on pages 94–96). Many of the newly discovered crystals work to harmonize the physical body with the lightbody, especially at the neural level.

While it is unwise to force the opening of these higher chakras before you are fully ready, you can prepare your body to receive the new influx of energy and the spiritual insights that accompany it. However, before this new energy can be of any benefit, you need to have worked on clearing any emotional blockages and limiting beliefs, letting go of karmic patterns and overcoming dis-ease. If you try to bypass any of this healing work, suppress issues or take short-cuts, you will end up ungrounded and open to illusions, delusions and misinformation because you will not be truly accessing the higher vibrational levels.

Brandenberg

Pink Petalite

Azeztulite

Phenacite

This exercise is suitable for Azeztulite, Elestial Smoky Quartz, blue-green Dioptase, pink Danburite, Tugtupeite, golden Danburite, Preseli Bluestone, Petalite, Nirvana Quartz, Phenacite, Brandenberg or other appropriate high-vibration crystals (see directory on pages 212–17).

Work with your crystals now To open the higher chakras, turn to Exercise 12: Bringing My Higher Chakras On-line on pages 108–9.

Note Undertake this exercise only when you have completed all your healing and therapeutic work.

I'm not quite there yet Continue to work on cleansing your chakras (see pages 98–99), releasing any emotional blocks you may have. If you are unsure about the position of the chakras, see the illustration on page 85, and check out their functions on pages 86–87.

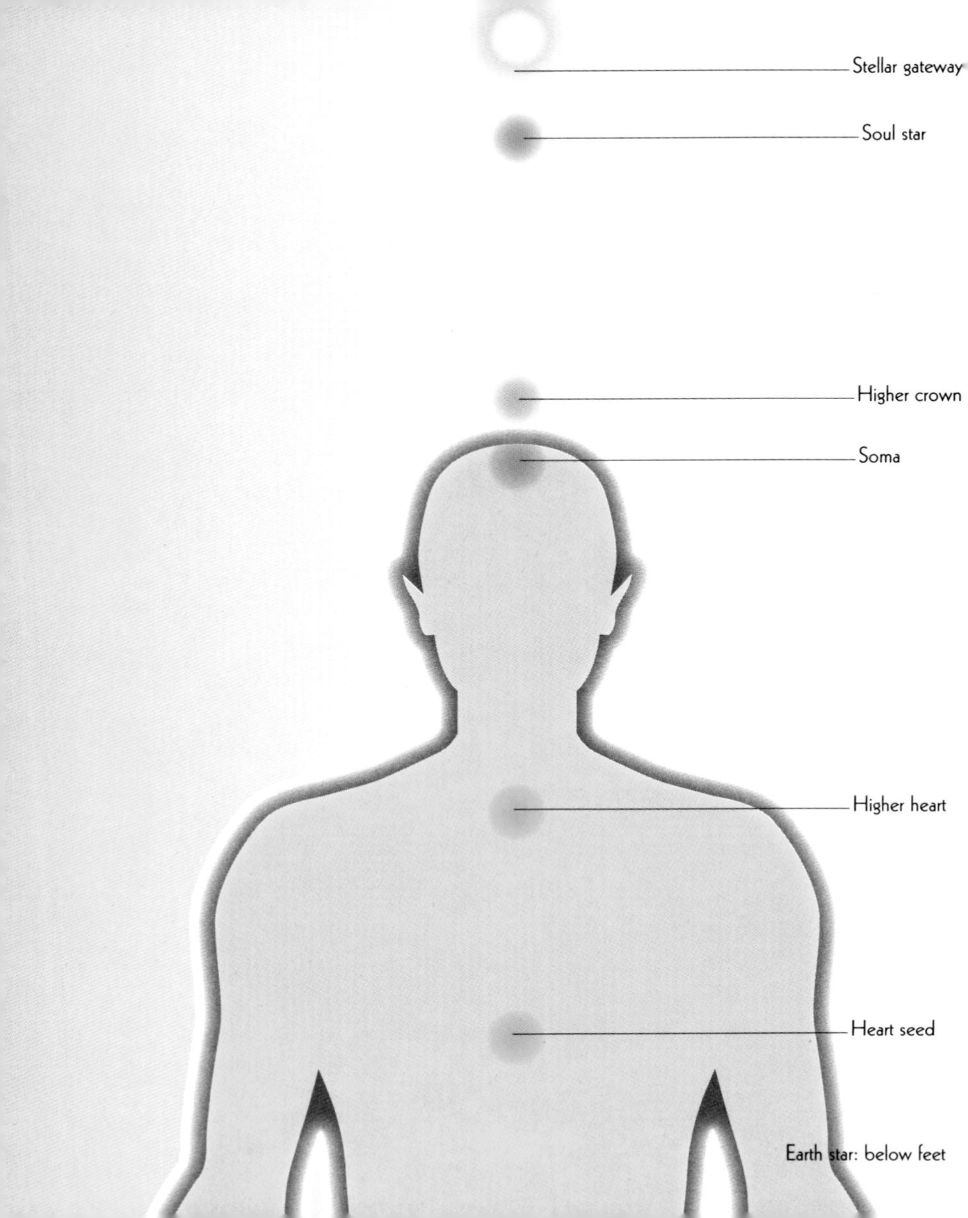
Stellar gateway
Soul star
Higher crown
Soma
Higher heart
Heart seed
Earth star: below feet

HIGHER VIBRATIONAL CHAKRAS

Earth star (higher earth)

COLOUR: Brown
POSITION: Below feet
ISSUE: Earth healing
POSITIVE QUALITIES: Grounded, connected to the earth's subtle grid, environmentally aware and a natural healer
NEGATIVE QUALITIES: Ungrounded, susceptible to environmental pollution, picks up negativity and creates disharmony

---

Heart seed

COLOUR: Pink
POSITION: Base of breastbone
ISSUE: Soul remembrance
POSITIVE QUALITIES: Remembrance of reason for incarnation, connection to divine plan and tools available to manifest potential
NEGATIVE QUALITIES: Rootless, purposeless, lost, spiritually disconnected, grieving, unable to express feelings, needy

Higher heart

COLOUR: Pink or blue-green
POSITION: Over thymus
ISSUE: Unconditional love
POSITIVE QUALITIES: Compassionate, empathic, nurturing, forgiving, spiritually connected
NEGATIVE QUALITIES: Cut off from spiritual nourishment and connectedness

---

Soma

COLOUR: Lavender-blue
POSITION: Centre of hairline
ISSUE: Spiritual connection
POSITIVE QUALITIES: Spiritually aware and fully conscious
NEGATIVE QUALITIES: Spaced-out and open to invasion, illusions and delusions

---

Higher crown

COLOUR: White
POSITION: Several above head
ISSUE: Spiritual enlightenment
POSITIVE QUALITIES: Spiritual, attuned to higher things, enlightened, truly humble
NEGATIVE QUALITIES: Fragmented soul, open to extra-terrestrial invasion

Soul star

COLOUR: Lavender/white
POSITION: 30 cm (1 foot) above head
ISSUE: Soul connection and highest self-illumination
POSITIVE QUALITIES: Ultimate soul connection, soul intertwining with physical body together with high-frequency light, communication with soul intention, objective perspective on past lifetimes
NEGATIVE QUALITIES: Invading, messiah-complex, rescues not empowers

Stellar gateway

COLOUR: White
POSITION: Above soul star chakra
ISSUE: Cosmic doorway to other worlds
POSITIVE QUALITIES: Connected to highest energies in the cosmos and beyond, in communication with enlightened beings
NEGATIVE QUALITIES: Disintegrated, open to cosmic disinformation, unable to function

CHAKRA EXERCISES

The following exercises will help you to sense and open your chakras and to keep them in good working order. They will also make you aware of your aura and activate the new higher vibration chakras when you are ready to do so.

Sensing and cleansing my chakras

Keeping your chakras balanced and active is essential for good health. You can either do a complete chakra cleanse and recharge, as described here, or you can just cleanse one chakra if you identify with a particular issue or the qualities detailed for that chakra on the chart on pages 84–87. Cleansing a single chakra is also useful if you have an illness or can feel a blockage associated with that chakra. Throat or lung conditions, for instance, respond if you treat the throat chakra, and abdominal distress the base or sacral chakra. For a quick cleanse, take a crystal wand or long point crystal and spiral the energy out from your chakra in one direction (such as clockwise) and then back in again (anti-clockwise). Cleanse the crystal in between if appropriate.

Exercise 9 FULL CHAKRA CLEANSE, BALANCE AND RECHARGE

AUDIO REFERENCE TRACK 3 (OPTIONAL)

- **You will need:** cleansed and activated Smoky Quartz, Red Jasper, Orange Carnelian, Yellow Jasper, Green Aventurine, Blue Lace Agate, Sodalite, Amethyst
- **Place the Smoky Quartz** between and slightly below your feet. Lie on your back. Visualize light and energy radiating out from the crystal into your earth chakra for two or three minutes. Be aware that the chakra is being cleansed and its spin regulated.
- **Place the Red Jasper on your base chakra.** Picture light and energy radiating out from the crystal into your base chakra, as before.

- **Place the Orange Carnelian on your sacral chakra**, just below the navel; again picture the light and feel the cleansing process.
- **Place the Yellow Jasper on your solar plexus**, the Green Aventurine on your heart, the Blue Lace Agate on your throat and the Sodalite on your brow. Each time, visualize the light and feel the cleansing at that chakra.
- **Lastly, place the Amethyst at the crown of your head** and see the light and feel the cleansing at your crown chakra.
- **Now guide your attention slowly from the soles of your feet** up the mid-line of your body, feeling how balanced and harmonized each chakra has become. Remain still and relaxed, inhaling deep into your belly and counting to seven before you exhale. As you breathe in and hold the breath, feel the energy of the crystals re-energizing the chakras and from there radiating out through your being.
- **When you feel ready, gather up your crystals**, starting from the crown. As you reach the earth chakra, be aware of a grounding cord anchoring you to the earth and into your physical body. Now cleanse your stones thoroughly and record your experiences in the space provided.

Chakra cleanse, balance and recharge

Date ______________________ **Time** ______________________

Crystals ______________________

Experience ______________________

Could I sense the energy in my chakras? ______________________

Were any chakras blocked? ______________________

Was I aware of any issues or illnesses associated with blocked or non-functioning chakras? (If so work further on this particular chakra later and report the experience here.) ______

If I used a long point crystal, how did it feel? ______

Chakras, crystals and colour

This exercise allows you to find out for yourself to which colours your chakras best respond and which colour they naturally exhibit. You can either practise with one of the regular chakras (see pages 82–87) at each session or you could work your way through the whole gamut if you have time.

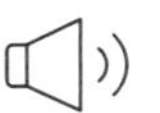

Exercise 10 WHAT COLOUR ARE MY CHAKRAS?

AUDIO REFERENCE TRACK 3 (OPTIONAL)

- **You will need:** a selection of cleansed and activated chakra crystals in different colours.
- **Turn back to pages 70–73 and remind yourself** how you responded to different-coloured crystals and whether any of your chakras reacted when you attuned to the various colours.
- **Relax and let your eyes go slightly** out of focus. Taking your attention to each chakra in turn, ask your intuition to tell you which colour each one is. You may see the answer as a colour or hear the word. (If you find this difficult, finger dowse the colour, see page 21.)
- **Working with each of the coloured crystals** in turn, hold a crystal close to one of your chakras, move it away and then bring it near your body again. Notice if this has any physical or subtle effect. Because chakras penetrate far out into the aura, check whether the colour changes or deepens the further you move the crystal away from your body.
- **Once you have established a colour** for each chakra, repeat the chakra cleanse and recharge from pages 98–101 with the new crystals, noticing what difference the colour of the crystal makes, if any.

What colours are my chakras?

Date ______________________ **Time** ______________________

Crystal ____

Chakra	**Colour**	**Effect**
Earth chakra		
Base chakra		
Sacral chakra		
Solar plexus chakra		
Heart chakra		
Higher heart chakra		
Throat chakra		
Brow chakra		
Crown chakra		

My experience ____

____

What was different about this experience? ____________________

____

Did my chakra colours deepen or change according to how far out in my aura they were? ______________________________

Did the chakra recharge feel better the first time I did it or when I changed the colours? ______________________________

Sensing and cleansing my aura

With the assistance of a crystal, you can easily train yourself to sense how far your aura extends and check it for weak spots or for hooks from other people who are pulling on your energy. Ask your intuition to show you which crystals would be appropriate to use. Carry out this exercise regularly.

Exercise 11 STRENGTHENING MY AURA

AUDIO REFERENCE TRACK 3 (OPTIONAL)

- **You will need**: cleansed and activated Smoky Quartz, Red Jasper, Labradorite, Clear Quartz or Selenite or other aura protection and cleansing crystal (see the Crystal Directory on pages 26–32)
- **Sit on a chair and place the Smoky Quartz** crystal at your feet (point facing outward if it has one). Place the Red Jasper on the chair beneath you, as close to your perineum as possible. Hold the Labradorite in your left hand and the Clear Quartz or Selenite in your right hand.
- **Close your eyes and breathe gently**, focusing your attention on your right hand. Extend your right arm to its full length with your palm facing into your body. Move your hand slowly toward your body. At some point your hand will start to tingle or the crystal will 'jump' and you will become aware of your subtle energy field. (This may take a little practice.)
- **Notice how far** the subtle energy field extends from your body. Move your right hand around to see if you can detect any 'cold' or weak spots. If you do, hold the crystal over the spot for a few moments.

- **Still holding the crystal** in your right hand, 'comb' your body from the top of your head down the front mid-line of your body to your feet. Repeat, combing down the outside of your body on each side and finally down your back.
- **Notice whether you feel any** 'hooks' or 'strings' that link your energy to that of someone else – these may be near your body or far out in the aura. If you do, use the crystal to dislodge the hook and send it back where it belongs, then heal the place where it was by holding the crystal over it. Notice too whether you are aware of any thoughts or feelings lodged in your aura and let the crystal gently dissolve these, too.
- **Repeat the 'combing'** using the Labradorite in your left hand; this strengthens and seals your aura. Finally, position the Clear Quartz in front of your solar plexus for a few minutes to energize your aura. Remember to cleanse the crystals after use and to record your experiences in the space provided.

My aura cleanse experience

Date ______________________ **Time** ______________________

Crystals ______________________

My experience ______________________

How did my aura feel? Did I discover any holes or breaks? ______________________

Were any thoughts or feelings lodged in my aura? ______________________

Were there any hooks from another person? ______________________

Did I remove all the thoughts, feelings and hooks? ______________________

My aura cleanse experience

Date ______________________ **Time** ______________________

Crystals ______________________

My experience ______________________

How did my aura feel? Did I discover any holes or breaks? ______________________

Were any thoughts or feelings lodged in my aura? ______________________

Were there any hooks from another person? ______________________

Did I remove all the thoughts, feelings and hooks? ______________________

Activating my higher chakras

This exercise helps you to bring your higher chakras 'on-line' when you are ready. Make sure that you work slowly and with thought. You may need to repeat the exercise several times before you feel the effect, and it is best not to push yourself. Rather, allow the process to unfold naturally when the time seems right. It can be beneficial to work on one chakra only per session until it is fully activated before moving onto the next one. Remember to close your chakras at the end of the exercise, if appropriate, by picturing shutters closing over them as you remove the crystal. If at any time you feel floaty, light-headed or dizzy, immediately remove the crystal, close the chakra and take your attention to the crystal at your feet. Re-anchor yourself by sensing your contact with the earth. Wait for a few days before you try the exercise again.

Exercise 12 BRINGING MY HIGHER CHAKRAS ON-LINE

AUDIO REFERENCE TRACK 3 (OPTIONAL)

- **You will need**: Elestial Smoky Quartz, blue Dioptase, pink Danburite, Tugtupeite, Danburite, Preseli Bluestone, Petalite, Nirvana Quartz, Phenacite, Brandenberg or other appropriate high-vibration crystals, such as Satyamani and Sayaloka Quartz or Tugtupeite (see the High-vibration Crystal Directory on pages 214–17)
- **Practise Exercise 9, the full chakra** cleanse, balance and recharge, on pages 98–99 to make sure that your traditional chakras are operating at their maximum efficiency and balance.
- **Place the piece of** Elestial Smoky Quartz or other high-vibration crystal between your feet to activate your higher earth chakra. Then place the blue Dioptase, pink Danburite or other high-vibration crystal over your higher heart

chakra. Wait for a few moments until the crystals and your chakra attune to each other and the chakra opens.

- **Place the Tugtupeite, Danburite** or other high-vibration crystal on the heart-seed chakra at the base of your breastbone. Wait for a few moments until the crystal and your chakra attune to each other and the chakra opens.
- **Place the Preseli Bluestone** or other high-vibration crystal on the soma chakra at your third eye. Wait for a few moments until the crystal and your chakra attune to each other and the chakra opens.
- **Place the Petalite, Nirvana Quartz** or other high-vibration crystal a hand's breadth above the crown of your head on the higher crown chakra. Wait for a few moments until the crystal and your chakra attune to each other and the chakra opens.
- **Place the Phenacite, Nirvana Quartz** or other high-vibration crystal about 30 cm (1 foot) above your head on the soul star chakra. Wait for a few moments until the crystal and your chakra attune to each other and the chakra opens.
- **Place a Brandenberg** or other high-dimension crystal on the stellar gateway above the soul star (see page 96). Wait for a few moments until the crystal and your chakra attune to each other and the chakra opens.
- **Close the chakras, if appropriate, by picturing shutters** closing over each chakra as you remove its crystal. Then picture a big bubble all around you, extending beneath your feet, and visualize the edges crystallizing to protect your newly active chakras. Now record your experiences in the space provided.

My higher chakras crystal activation experience

Date ______________________ **Time** ______________________

Crystal ______________________ **Chakra** ______________________

My experience ______________________

____

____

The most appropriate crystals for me were ______________________

____

____

____

Date ______________________ **Time** ______________________

Crystal ______________________ **Chakra** ______________________

My experience ______________________

____

____

The most appropriate crystals for me were ______________________

____

____

____

My higher chakras crystal activation experience

Date ______________________ **Time** ______________________

Crystal ______________________ **Chakra** ______________________

My experience ______________________

____

____

The most appropriate crystals for me were ______________________

____

____

____

Date ______________________ **Time** ______________________

Crystal ______________________ **Chakra** ______________________

My experience ______________________

____

____

The most appropriate crystals for me were ______________________

____

____

____

My higher chakras crystal activation experience

Date ______________________ **Time** ______________________

Crystal ______________________ **Chakra** ______________________

My experience ______________________

The most appropriate crystals for me were ______________________

Date ______________________ **Time** ______________________

Crystal ______________________ **Chakra** ______________________

My experience ______________________

The most appropriate crystals for me were ______________________

CRYSTALS FOR SELF-DEVELOPMENT

Crystal qualities

In addition to their healing properties, many crystals can offer you support if you would like to nurture specific qualities to benefit your personal development. If you would like to develop more compassion, for example, then wearing, meditating or sleeping with a Rose Quartz or another heart stone will be of help. If you need to develop more courage, pop a suitably programmed Red Jasper or Red Carnelian into your pocket. If you suffer from anger and need to calm down, avoid red crystals and go for cool pink or green stones, such as Aventurine or Jade. If you constantly criticize yourself, Tiger's Eye can help, and if you are sensitive to criticism Citrine assists, while Kunzite shows how to act on constructive criticism.

You may already be using crystals in this way unconsciously. Many people intuitively or deliberately place crystals over their chakras to release blockages (see pages 82–87) and allow positive qualities to manifest. Look through your crystal collection now – you may find that a number of stones all offer you the same quality, which is evidence that your intuition has drawn you to the right remedy. If this is the case, consciously programme the crystal to bring you more of the quality you are seeking (see pages 22–23), then wear the crystal or sleep with it under your pillow for several weeks. From time to time monitor how you are feeling to check whether you need to move on to a different crystal.

Knowing yourself is one of the secrets of a happy and successful life and a Quartz crystal, or any crystal to which you are intuitively drawn, can help you to explore your inner self and the contents of the more hidden parts of your psyche. The crystal shown here, for instance, revealed a troubled childhood and difficult early adulthood, but the phantom and the rainbow at the top pointed the way to happiness and spiritual evolution, drawing on the inner strength developed during those early difficulties.

This exercise is suitable for Any crystal to which you are attracted or that offers you the qualities you are seeking to develop.

Work with your crystals now Turn to Exercise 13: My Quartz Crystal Journey on page 130, remembering to prepare your crystal before you begin (see pages 22–23). The journey can be made in several parts if you wish.

I'm not quite there yet Look up the qualities of the crystals to which you are intuitively attracted in the Crystal Directory on pages 26–32 and see what they tell you about yourself. Alternatively, check out your chakras and the qualities they are associated with on pages 84–87.

Which crystals do I love?

The crystals that you love say a great deal about your personality and your approach to life, and it can be extremely insightful to re-read information on the properties of the crystals in your collection (see the Crystal Directory on pages 26–32) or to think about the type of crystal you tend to go for. If you always pick big, bright and shiny crystals, for example, you are probably optimistic and outgoing – or you might be trying to overcome the needy child element of yourself who wants to feel better by handling pretty, sparkly things.

If all your crystals are a particular colour, you may be trying to strengthen the chakra or qualities associated with that colour. Light colours can indicate a seeker after spiritual evolution or someone who avoids shadow qualities. If you opt for deep, dark and intense crystals, you are probably using them to transform your shadow qualities into gifts or protecting yourself against negative thoughts and feelings that may come from outside yourself.

Looking deeply into the qualities of the crystals to which you are attracted is an excellent way to learn more about the unconscious urges you harbour within yourself and to develop the positive side of your personality.

This exercise is suitable for Any crystal to which you are attracted or which you wear regularly.

Work with your crystals now To learn what the crystals to which you are attracted say about you, turn to Exercise 14: What Do the Crystals I Love Tell Me? on page 134.

I'm not quite there yet Study the properties of the crystals in your collection further.

The crystals you choose to wear say a great deal about your personality.

Which crystals do I avoid?

There are two main reasons for avoiding particular crystals (apart from cost): either you don't like the look of the crystal or you have responded badly when wearing or handling one previously. This could be a clue to something you are trying to hide from yourself. It might be a feeling or an attitude you deem to be 'bad' and have suppressed deep within your subconscious, or perhaps the crystal is having a cathartic or detoxifying effect that is a little too strong for you. In either case, allowing yourself to explore the cause of your aversion and gently drawing off the feelings with a crystal such as Smoky Quartz will make you feel much better. Once you have drawn off the initial source of distress, you may require the support of a crystal that instils the opposite quality.

The Smoky Elestial crystal pictured opposite was deeply disliked by one of my workshop participants – she said it looked like 'an angry snake waiting to pounce'. Having worked with the crystal, she realized that it was bringing back the memory of a flasher jumping out of the bushes when she was a small child. Smoky Elestial Quartz is a beautiful crystal for transmuting the depression and fear such a traumatic memory can cause, and it reminded her that her gift of swift feet had carried her to safety.

This exercise is suitable for Any crystal to which you have an aversion or any traumatic memory you wish to release.

Work with your crystals now To learn how you can bring hidden memories and traumatic or undesirable feelings to the surface for release, turn to Exercise 15: Facing My Shadow Energy on pages 138–39.

I'm not quite there yet Sit quietly holding one of the 'soft' crystals, such as Rose Quartz or Rhodochrosite, that dispel fear until you feel able to work with the avoided crystal.

How can I protect myself with crystals?

Psychic self-protection is essential if you are to work sensibly with crystals – and for other reasons too. Other people's energies and thoughts can quickly deplete your energy. Electromagnetic smog and geopathic stress also affect how well you can work with your crystals because, if you don't take steps to prevent it, you can pick them up as negative energies that lodge in your aura or your organs. Family members or partners can also create stress in each other. So, what do you do about it?

Well, crystals are brilliant at providing protection and creating safe spaces, drawing off negative energies and keeping energy pirates at bay. By keeping your energy as high as possible, you will also be able to attune to high-vibration crystals when you are ready, raising your own vibrations to reach multi-dimensional spaces.

Remember when seeking protection from crystals to cleanse them regularly, especially if you are wearing them or they are out in your environment (see pages 22–23). Also, be aware that you can wear or place crystals to block negative energies from reaching you. For example, placing crystals such as Rose Quartz or Labradorite near a party wall if you have noisy or intrusive neighbours calms them down almost immediately. Wearing a Black Tourmaline when you've annoyed someone or are the object of their jealousy protects you, absorbing ill-wishing and bringing peace to your life once more.

The spleen protector

If you feel exhausted in someone's company, or wilt when she or he phones you – especially if you have an ache under your left armpit – then this person is drawing on your energy field via your spleen chakra.

You will find that a spleen protector soon sorts out such energy pirates, and, as a general rule, green crystals, such as Jade, Fluorite and Gaspeite, work well for the spleen chakra. There are other crystals that can be used to provide similar protection for your solar plexus (protecting you from emotional draining), your liver (from other people's anger invading you), your kidneys (from other people's fear invading you) and so on.

This exercise is suitable for Any form of energy depletion you experience; choose your crystal by intuition or from the references in the Crystal Directory on pages 26–32.

Work with your crystals now To cut off energy drains, turn to Exercise 16: Protecting My Spleen on page 140.

I'm not quite there yet Play Track 1 of the audio, relax and take your mind back to situations in which you always feel tired or experience sudden energy depletion. This will help you to identify energy pirates and adverse situations.

DIRECTORY OF PROTECTION CRYSTALS

Fluorite, Amazonite or Quartz Neutralize electromagnetic smog; place clusters by the computer or TV.

Green Fluorite

Smoky Quartz Absorbs geopathic stress and negative energies of all kinds and protects against energy drains.

Smoky Quartz

Turquoise Clears environmental pollution and assists personal protection.

Turquoise

Labradorite Separates your energy from other people's thoughts and feelings so that you are able to retain an empathetic yet objective perceptive viewpoint.

Labradorite

Black Tourmaline

Black Tourmaline Deflects ill-wishing and protects against electromagnetic smog; tape one to your mobile phone.

Sodalite

Green Aventurine and Sodalite Protect against electromagnetic smog.

Bloodstone

Amber or Bloodstone Cleanse negative energies and protect the aura.

Selenite

Selenite Draws spiritual energies to create a safe, sacred space.

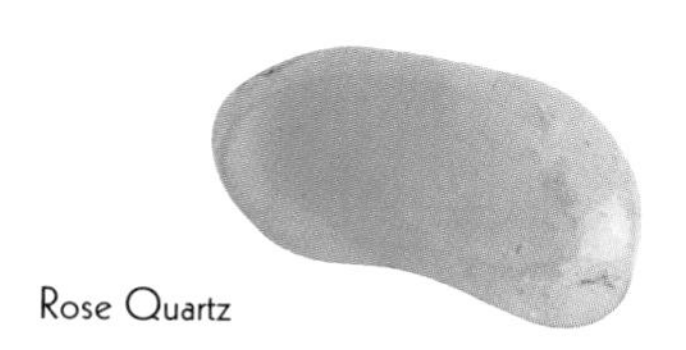

Rose Quartz

Rose Quartz or Amethyst Replace negativity with positive, loving vibrations; place against the wall to calm intrusive energies or emotional angst.

Protecting my space

Crystal grids are the perfect way to safeguard your space because they create an energetic net. They also create a safe holding space while you journey or conduct rituals. In fact, by positioning your crystals in ordered grids rather than placing them randomly, you can enhance all your space, by keeping the areas cleansed and energized.

There are many shapes of grid, so experiment with them in order to work out which one makes you feel good. Experiment too with the crystals you use. Dowsing is an excellent way to both choose and position your crystals (see pages 20–21).

Remember that crystals used in this way require regular cleansing. After cleansing them, re-connect them using a wand. (If the gridlines pass through a wall, take the wand up to the wall and then around to the other side, where the line continues.)

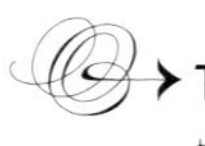

This exercise is suitable for All protective crystals, but especially those on page 123.

Work with your crystals now To check out which grids are beneficial for you, turn to Exercise 17: Using Grid Systems on page 142. Select the stones and their exact positioning by finger or pendulum dowsing.

I'm not quite there yet Check out the protective properties of crystals in the Crystal Directory on pages 26–32 and then revise your finger-dowsing technique (see page 21).

Dowsing pendulum

CRYSTAL GRIDS

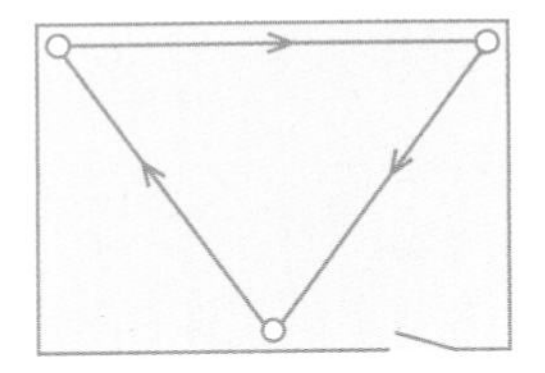

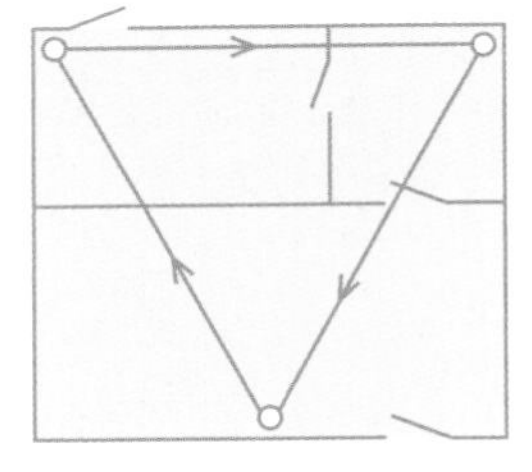

Triangulation

You will need:

- 3 cleansed and activated crystals
- Crystal wand

Triangulation gridding works well to neutralize negative energy and bring in positive energy. Place one crystal centrally along a wall and two others on the wall opposite at an equal angle if possible. If you are working on a whole house, the lines of force pass through walls, so connect the points with a wand to strengthen the grid.

Zig-zag

You will need:

- 8 cleansed and activated crystals
- Crystal wand

The zig-zag layout is particularly useful for dealing with sick building syndrome and environmental pollution. Place appropriate crystals as shown on the diagram, remembering to return from the last stone laid to the first. Cleanse the stones regularly.

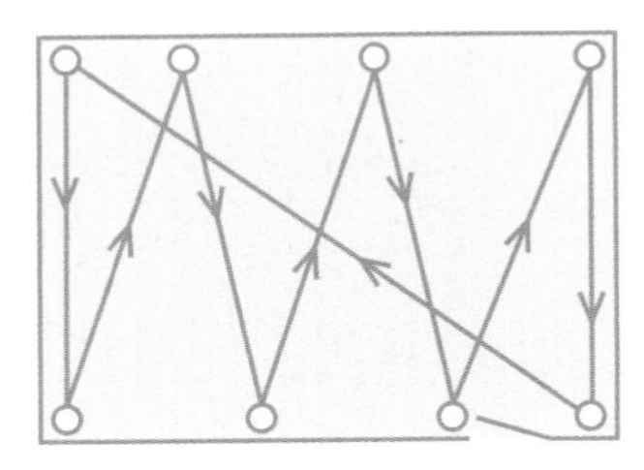

Five-pointed star

You will need:

- 5 cleansed and activated stones
- Crystal wand

This is a useful protection layout or caller-in of love and healing, and it enhances your energy. Follow the direction of the arrows on the diagram when placing crystals and remember to return to the start crystal to complete the circuit. Like the Star of David (see page 128), this layout can be used to grid around a body and also for a room or other space.

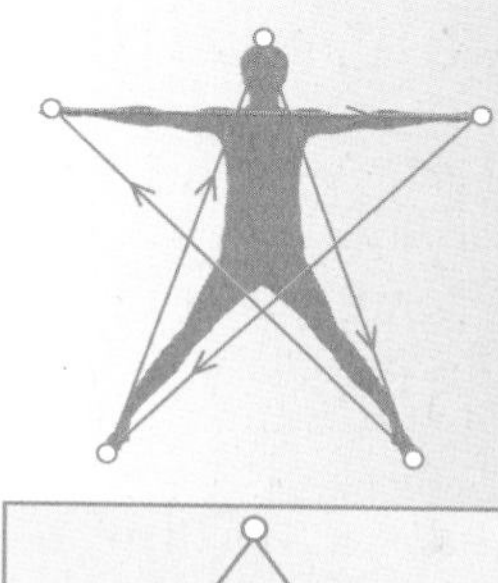

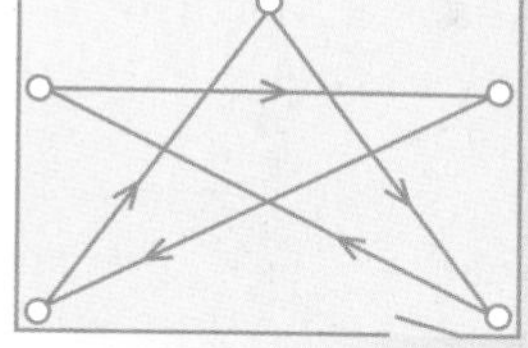

Figure-of-eight

You will need:

- 6 cleansed and activated high-vibration stones
- 6 cleansed and activated grounding stones

This layout draws spiritual energy down into the body and melds it with earth energy drawn up from the feet to create perfect balance. It also opens a cosmic anchor to ground you between the core of the earth and the galactic centre, creating core-energy solidity that equips you to ride out energetic changes and channel high-vibration energy down to earth. Place high-vibration stones, such as Amphibole, Cacoxenite and Blue Moonstone, above the waist to the crown of the head, and grounding stones, such as Poppy Jasper, Agate and Septarian, below the waist, down to the feet. Remember to complete the circuit back to the first stone that you placed.

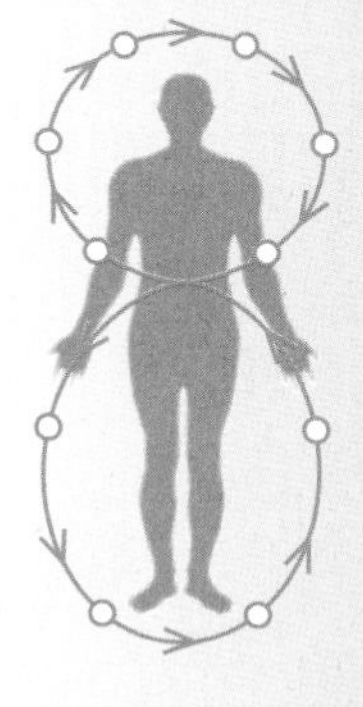

Star of David

You will need:

- 6 cleansed and activated crystals
- Crystal wand

The Star of David is a traditional protection layout but it also creates an ideal manifestation space when it is laid with large Grossular Garnet, Ammolite or other abundance stones. Lay the first triangle and join up the points, then lay another triangle the other way up, over the top. Join up the points. If you are using Bronzite and Black Tourmaline to neutralize ill-wishing, lay the Bronzite triangle first and cleanse the star daily.

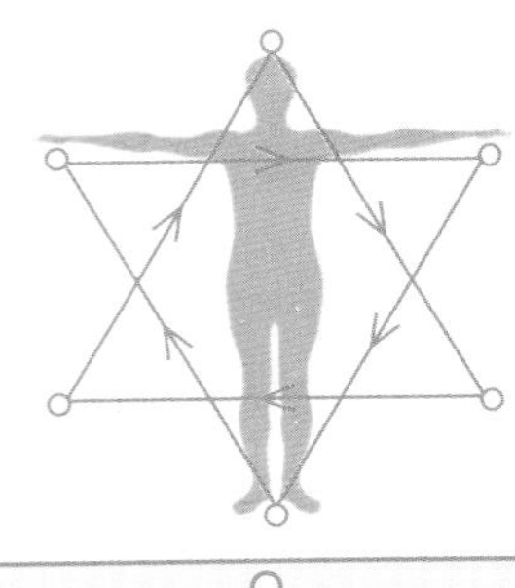

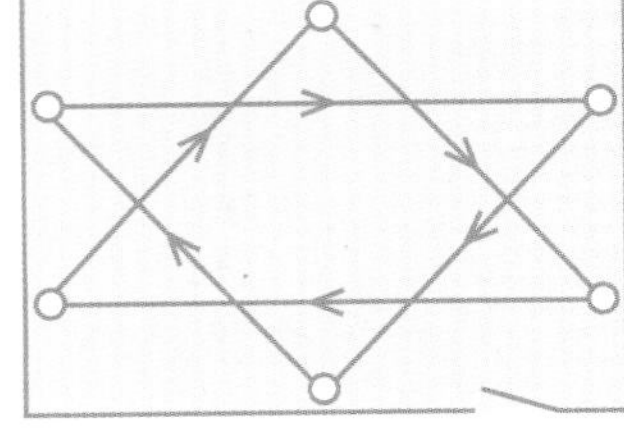

SELF-DEVELOPMENT EXERCISES

The exercises in this section will help you to raise your vibrations and enhance your sensitivity to crystals while encouraging you to take on new qualities that support your self-development. They also assist you in keeping your personal and environmental energies high, clean and safe.

What can crystals tell me about myself?

This journey takes you deep inside yourself to experience your ego and your unique sense of self. You will find out what makes you *you* and how you can express your individuality. The journey then moves you out to see how you fit into the wider picture. This helps you to harness your ability to innovate, to lead and to follow your own path with courage. This journey can be undertaken in shorter sections if you find it too much to do at one time. Simply pause the audio when you need to, but always follow the close-down at the end each time you complete a section and remember to date your experience.

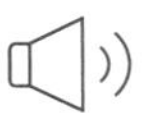

Exercise 13 MY QUARTZ CRYSTAL JOURNEY

AUDIO REFERENCE TRACK 4 (TO FOLLOW THE SCRIPT, TURN TO PAGES 246–247)

- **You will need**: a cleansed and activated crystal intuitively selected from your crystal collection; a Quartz crystal is ideal, but be guided by your intuition
- **Play Track 4 of the audio now** and follow the instructions for your Quartz crystal journey. After completing your journey, record your experience in the space provided.

My Quartz crystal journey experience

Date ______________________ **Time** ______________________

Crystal ______________________

My experience ______________________

What drives my ego and my desires? ______________________

How do I assert myself? ______________________

How do I express this in my day-to-day life? ______________________

What areas of life do I procrastinate in?

Where am I totally self-absorbed?

What is the difference between my ego and my Self?

What was it like to be part of the whole and then to become a unique individual again?

How did it feel to birth my Self? ____________________

What is my pathway? ____________________

What were the gifts in my shadow? ____________________

What were the gifts I left for myself? ____________________

What do my crystals tell me?

If it contains a preponderance of certain colours or types of crystal, then your crystal collection may say a great deal about the type of qualities you value or are trying to attract to yourself. This exercise will help you to explore this.

Exercise 14 WHAT DO THE CRYSTALS I LOVE TELL ME?

- **You will need:** 4 or 5 cleansed and activated crystals of various shapes and/or colours
- **Take a close look** at your crystal collection. If it contains several crystals of one particular colour, turn to page 88 and check out which chakra this colour resonates with, then look at pages 86–87 to find out which qualities and characteristics are associated with that chakra
- **Now turn to the Crystal Directory** on pages 26–32 or *The Crystal Bible* and read about the qualities of all your favourite crystals. Does a common theme run through the descriptions? If so, what does this say about you?
- **Look at the crystals illustrated** on page 117. Which pendant would you like to wear? Read on to find out what this says about you: Mystic Topaz is optimistic and outgoing and likes to dazzle; Merlinite is restrained, discerning and self-contained; Blue Moonstone is mystical and intuitive; Greenlandite is dependable and calm; Lemurian Jade is protective and mysterious. Now record your experience in the space provided.

My crystal collection experience

Date ______________________ **Time** ______________________

Crystals ______________________

My experience ______________________

Did a particular colour or theme run through my crystals?

Did my crystals tie into a particular chakra?

If so, having read the qualities associated with that chakra, how does this apply to me either positively or negatively?

What positive qualities do my crystals bring to me?

Which crystal particularly attracted me on the illustration?

What were its properties?

Overcoming aversion

This exercise can be carried out with any crystal to which you feel an aversion or you can work with a crystal that you have identified as representing one of your particular fears or issues. The crystals placed at your feet, such as Smoky Quartz or Hematite, help to draw off and detoxify traumatic feelings or memories. You can also hold Rose Quartz to calm your fear.

Exercise 15 FACING MY SHADOW ENERGY

- **You will need:** A crystal to which you have an aversion, Smoky Quartz or Hematite (if you have an aversion to these crystals, substitute clear Quartz), plus a heart-healing crystal or one that instils the positive side of the aversion (see the Crystal Directory on pages 26–32)
- **Place the Smoky Quartz or Hematite** (or clear Quartz) between your feet.
- **Now hold the crystal to which you** have an aversion; if the aversion is really strong, place the stone on a table in front of you. Ask yourself what it is you dislike so much about this stone. Is it the colour? The shape? The feelings you get when you look at it? Ask yourself where you feel the aversion: in your hands, your heart or your gut? Does it make you feel sick or your back squirm?
- **Breathe gently and calmly, taking the breath** right down into your belly. Ask the crystal to talk to you – to communicate with you to help you identify where this aversion stems from inside yourself. What memories does it bring up or which attitudes does it represent? Ask the crystal to help you gently release and heal these negative feelings.
- **When you have finished exploring** the negative feelings, take the heart-healing or postive crystal and hold it over your heart. Breathe gently into the crystal so that

the energy flows into your heart. Tap the crystal gently over your heart and repeat to yourself several times, 'I forgive myself for having this feeling/memory/aversion, and I unconditionally love and accept myself for having had it. I release myself now.' Now write up your experience in the space provided.

My crystal aversion experience

Date ______________ **Time** ______________ **Crystal** ______________

My experience ______________________________

____

____

What the crystal symbolized ______________________________

____

Crystals used to heal it ______________________________

____

How I feel now ______________________________

____

____

Protecting myself

Crystallizing the outer edges of your aura, provides some protection from energy pirates and other sappers of your subtle energy, but to further ensure that no one can pull on your energy, use this exercise to protect your spleen. Experiment with the different crystals mentioned until you find exactly the right one for you and, if you suffer from extreme energy depletion, keep the stone taped over your spleen.

Exercise 16 PROTECTING MY SPLEEN

- **You will need:** Green Fluorite, Green Aventurine, Jade or other spleen crystal, plus Quantum Quattro or another power stone (see pages 214–17)
- **Tape one of the crystals** over your spleen chakra (about a hand's breadth beneath your left armpit). This immediately cuts off hooks from energy pirates.
- **Now picture a large**, three-dimensional pyramid extending down from the spleen chakra just below your left armpit to your waist on the back and front of your body. Give the pyramid a floor. This will protect your spleen further.
- **To re-empower yourself,** replace the crystal with the Quantum Quattro or one of the other power stones.
- **To protect yourself in other ways**, repeat the crystal-and-pyramid set-up using red crystals over your liver (for protection from other people's anger), yellow crystals over your solar plexus (for protection from those desperate for emotional nourishment), or green or pink crystals over your heart (protection against picking up someone's heartbreak). Now record your experience in the space provided.

My spleen protection experience

Date ______________________ **Time** ______________________

Crystals ______________________

My experience ______________________

The best crystal to protect my spleen was ______________________

The best crystal to protect my liver was ______________________

The best crystal to protect my solar plexus was ______________________

The best crystal to protect my heart was ______________________

Protecting my environment

Carefully positioning crystals into a grid provides you with a safe, peaceful and energetically clean space in which to live, love, work, play and meditate. Remember to join the crystals with a wand to complete the grid.

Exercise 17 USING GRID SYSTEMS

- **You will need:** a selection of protective gridding crystals (see pages 126–28), plus a wand
- **Study the grids on pages 126–128** to find out which shape you intuitively respond to. Begin by laying out that grid on the floor, as shown. Join up the crystals with the wand and then stand in the centre to see how the grid feels.
- **Try out all the grids in turn,** varying the crystals as appropriate.
- **When you find the grid and crystals** that resonate best with your energies, lay that grid around your home, room or workspace and leave it in place. Now record your experience in the space provided.

My crystal gridding experience

Date ______________________ **Time** ______________________

Crystals ______________________

Grid shape ______________________

Effect on me ______________________

____

Date ______________________ **Time** ______________________

Crystals ______________________

Grid shape ______________________

Effect on me ______________________

____

Date ______________________ **Time** ______________________

Crystals ______________________

Grid shape ______________________

Effect on me ______________________

____

Date ______________________ **Time** ______________________

Crystals ______________________

____

Grid shape ______________________

Effect on me ______________________

____

Date ______________________ **Time** ______________________

Crystals ______________________

____

Grid shape ______________________

Effect on me ______________________

____

Date ______________________ **Time** ______________________

Crystals ______________________

____

Grid shape ______________________

Effect on me ______________________

____

HOW CAN I BE MY OWN CRYSTAL HEALER?

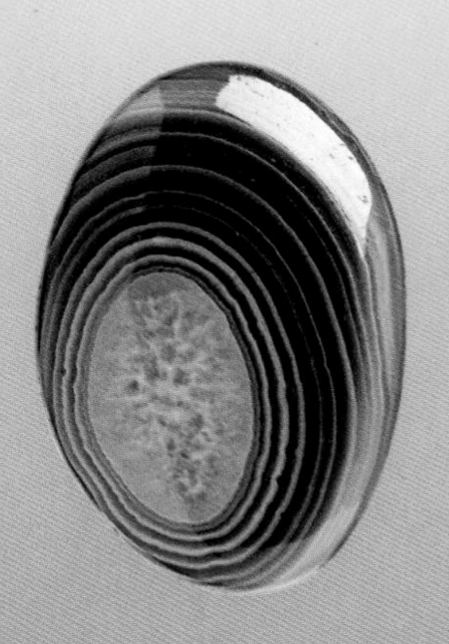

Sources of dis-ease

Dis-ease is a state of disequilibrium that results from physical imbalances, blocked feelings, suppressed emotions, toxic thoughts or environmental stress (caused by excess electromagnetic stimulation or 'sick building syndrome'). If left unchecked, dis-ease can finally result in physical illness. Because healing means bringing back into balance, crystals are an excellent way to treat dis-ease, since they gently correct imbalances in the body, emotions, mind, aura and the chakras (see pages 82–87).

Everyone has the potential to be a crystal healer, and it is easy to stimulate your own self-healing by placing crystals on or around your body. This can include wearing a crystal for long periods of time, or placing or taping a crystal over an organ for a shorter period.

The immune system

Your first lines of defence against the invasion of dis-ease and organisms such as viruses or bacteria are your physical and psychic immune systems. Lack of balance in the physical immune system can lead to illness. If this system is underactive, for example, viral infections such as colds and flu may result. If it is overactive, you could be prone to rheumatoid arthritis or lupus. A dysfunctional physical immune system is a common response to environmental, emotional, mental or physical stress. A disturbance in the psychic immune system is usually caused by toxic emotions or thoughts or by ill-wishing, negative environmental energies and blocked chakras.

To discover whether your immune systems are out of balance, you can dowse (see pages 20–21) or judge for yourself the reaction of your immune system to a specific crystal. Then you can restore balance by stimulating or calming both your immune systems via the thymus gland, situated in the centre of your chest, about a hand's breadth below your collarbone. To enhance your physical immune system, place a piece of Smithsonite at each corner of your bed and tape a Green Tourmaline or Bloodstone over your thymus, leaving it in place overnight. To enhance your psychic immune system, try placing Black Tourmaline, Brandenberg Amethyst or Selenite over your thymus.

Immune stimulators

Environmental stress Bloodstone, Smithsonite, Amethyst, Clear Quartz, Green Aventurine

Emotional stress Rose Quartz, Danburite

Mental stress Sodalite, Green Tourmaline

Viruses Fluorite, Cathedral Quartz, Amphilbole

Auto-immune system Paraiba or other Tourmaline

Make a note of any other crystals that you find effective in the exercises that accompany this chapter.

This exercise is suitable for Any of the crystals mentioned above or which you intuitively choose.

Work with your crystals now To explore the effect of crystals on your immune system turn to Exercise 18: Finding My Immune-system Crystal on pages 162–63.

I'm not quite there yet Turn to pages 82–87 to revise the information on crystals and the chakras, or turn to pages 152–57 to find out about crystals and the organs.

Crystals and my emotions

Using crystals is an excellent way to balance your moods and transmute negative emotions into positive ones. So often the dis-ease is caused by toxic emotions and repressed feelings that we unwittingly hold onto when they are long past their 'sell-by date'. Since these emotions are so deep, we have no idea what is causing our inner distress. Crystals winkle out these hidden vulnerabilities, gently bringing them to our attention and showing us how to find the gift held within them – the signpost to emotional well-being.

Toxic emotions can be held within the heart, the chakras or aura, and so placing appropriate crystals on these points is extremely beneficial. You may need to repeat the placement daily or to tape the crystals in place for several days while the underlying cause of the dis-ease surfaces. Then you may require another crystal to help you heal – you can intuitively finger dowse this crystal (see page 21) or read up on the properties of the crystals detailed in the Crystal Directory on pages 26–32 or in either volume of *The Crystal Bible*. You can also use Gem Essences (see pages 190–92) to heal emotional dis-ease.

This is by no means a definitive list of healing crystals for the emotions, but it will help you to start turning your emotional dis-ease into emotional well-being. Make a note of other crystals you find effective in the exercises that accompany this chapter.

HEALING CRYSTALS FOR EMOTIONS

Powerlessness
CHAKRA: Earth
CRYSTAL: Smoky Quartz
POSITIVE EMOTION: Empowerment

Insecurity
CHAKRA: Base
CRYSTAL: Red Jasper
POSITIVE EMOTION: Security

Low self-esteem
CHAKRA: Sacral
CRYSTAL: Orange Carnelian
POSITIVE EMOTION: Self-confidence

Inferiority
CHAKRA: Solar plexus
CRYSTAL: Yellow Jasper
POSITIVE EMOTION: Empathy

Resentment
CHAKRA: Base and Heart
CRYSTAL: Rhodorite
POSITIVE EMOTION: Appreciation

Jealousy
CHAKRA: Heart
CRYSTAL: Green Aventurine
POSITIVE EMOTION: Compassion

Neediness
CHAKRA: Higher heart
CRYSTAL: Rose Quartz
POSITIVE EMOTION: Unconditional love

Disloyalty
CHAKRA: Throat
CRYSTAL: Blue Lace Agate
POSITIVE EMOTION: Loyalty

Self-delusion
CHAKRA: Brow
CRYSTAL: Sodalite
POSITIVE EMOTION: Emotional clarity

Arrogance
CHAKRA: Crown
CRYSTAL: Clear Quartz
POSITIVE EMOTION: Joy

Releasing from the past

Do you have any Rainbow Obsidian or any other banded crystal among the crystals in your collection? If so, you have selected the perfect tool to release yourself from the past. You intuitively chose this crystal because you are holding onto something that is detrimental to your current well-being and because this crystal will offer insight into the gifts that lie at the heart of the situation.

If your lover has left you and you are having difficulty letting go, for instance, wearing beautiful Rainbow Obsidian or Rhodochrosite over your heart will sever the cords of old love, encouraging you to move on. These crystals help you to recognize the lessons you have learned, the inner strengths you have drawn on, and the qualities you have developed during the relationship. If you have things to say that you never dared say before, feelings to express or creative energy to manifest, then gentle Blue Lace Agate can assist you.

Any banded crystal is perfect for facilitating such a journey of self-discovery. While undertaking the journey deep into your self you may see clear pictures, experience physical or emotional feelings, or simply *know*, and insights become clearer as you write them down, so keep a record in the journal section of this book.

Blue Lace Agate

Malachite

Banded Agate

Rainbow Obsidian

This journey is suitable for Banded or Whorled Jaspers, Banded Agate, Botswana Agate, Blue Lace Agate, Tiger's Eye, Hawk Eye, Malachite, Rhodochrosite, Phantom Quartzes, Ammolite, Chrysotile, Shaman Quartz, Charoite, Nebula Stone, Rhyolite, Sugilite; assessing the properties of any whorled or banded crystal.

Work with your crystals now Turn to Exercise 19: My Rainbow Obsidian Journey on page 166, remembering to prepare your crystal before you begin (see pages 22–23). The journey can be made in several parts if you wish.

I'm not quite there yet If you don't feel tuned into a healing crystal, go to Exercise 4: Attuning to My Crystals on pages 44–45.

Crystals and my organs

Many crystals resonate with specific body organs and can be used to support healing and to bring an organ back into balance. You can either place the crystal over the chakra closest to the organ or over the organ itself, then leave it in place for 15–20 minutes. Crystal layouts can also be extremely useful for detoxifying your organs (see page 170).

Much early crystal healing came about because of notions of similarity and correspondence: stones that looked like an organ or a condition were used to cure it. Bloodstone, which is green and red, has been used for 5,000 years to heal the blood and blood-rich organs and to strengthen the kidneys. It is still used today, like Snakeskin Agate, a very wrinkled crystal used to overcome skin conditions.

Physical and subtle anatomy

Knowing where your organs lie within your body allows you to position crystals for maximum effect. If you already know about the body's energy meridian systems you can also utilize these for crystal healing.

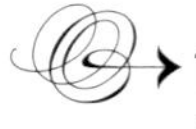

This exercise is suitable for Bloodstone, Amethyst, Red Jasper, Smoky Quartz, Sodalite, Yellow Jasper and other detoxing stones.

Work with your crystals now To experience a crystal detox, turn to Exercise 20: My Detox Layout on page 170.

I'm not quite there yet Study the physical anatomy diagram opposite to learn where your organs are, or turn to pages 82–87 to check out your chakras and make sure there are no blockages.

Physical anatomy

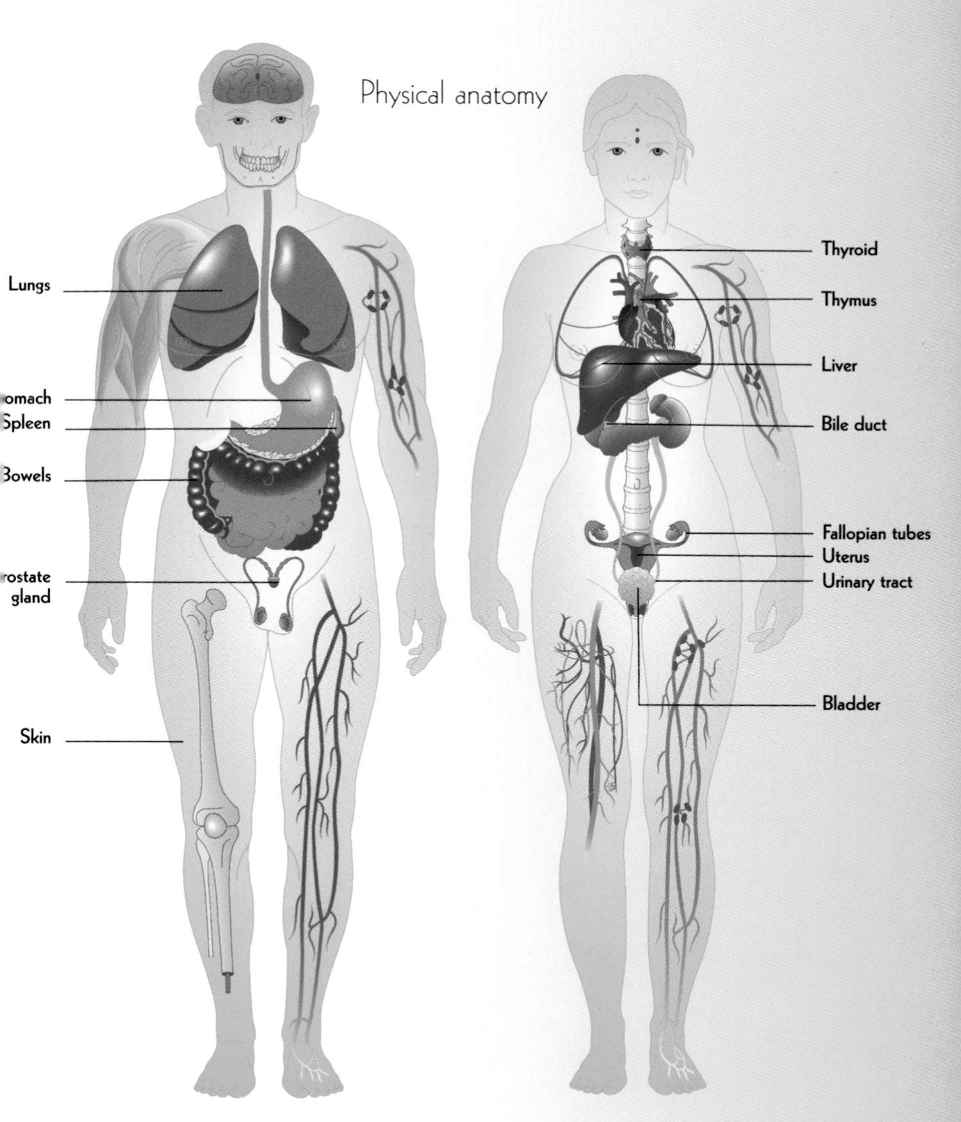

Subtle anatomy

The various layers of the aura interweave and may appear as different colours to an intuitive eye.

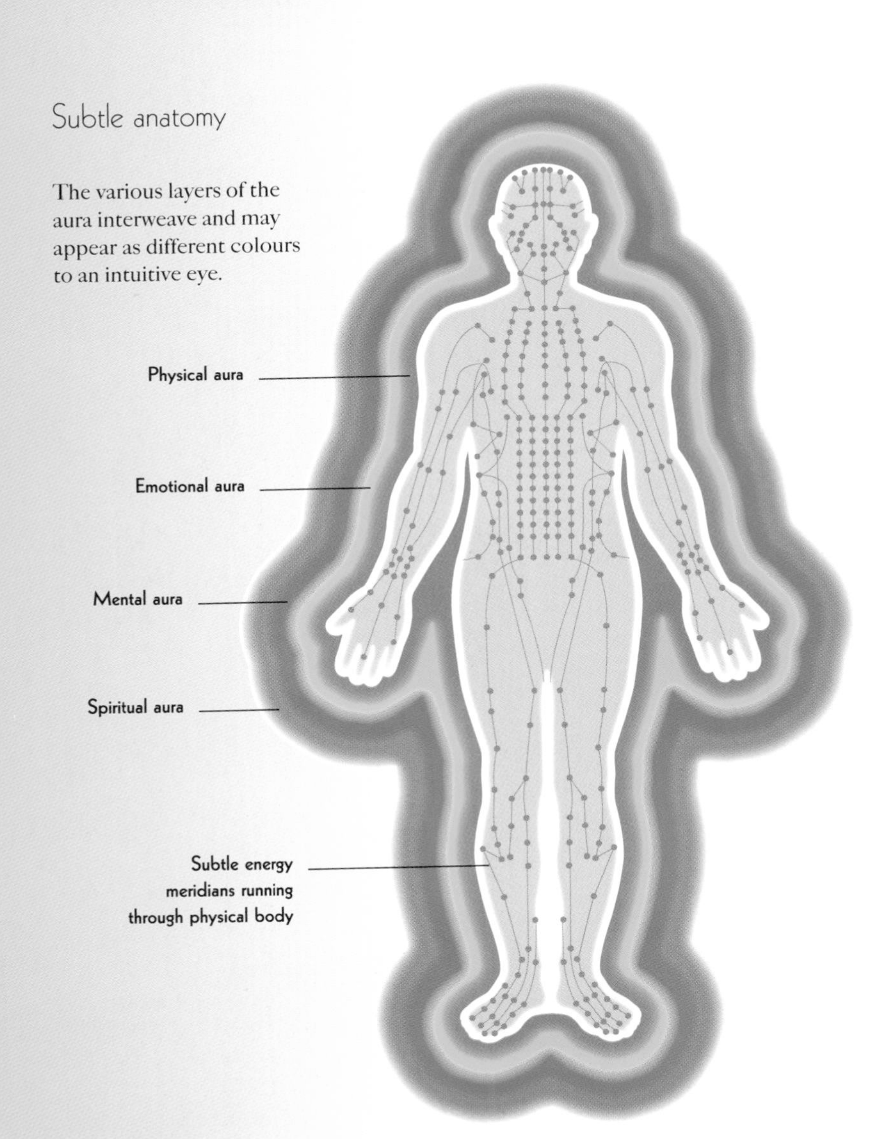

THE DETOXIFICATION LAYOUT

If your body is overloaded with toxins it cannot maintain good health. Stimulating your liver by using the detoxification layout releases toxins and encourages your lymphatic system to remove them, bringing about a physical cleansing. Placing a Yellow Jasper on your solar plexus brings about an emotional detox as well, while if you feel that your mind needs detoxing, add crystals such as Fluorite or Sodalite.

You can adapt the detoxification layout given on page 170 to work on different organs by changing the crystals. Choose those that correspond with the organ you wish to rebalance by looking at the list on pages 156–57 and position them appropriately.

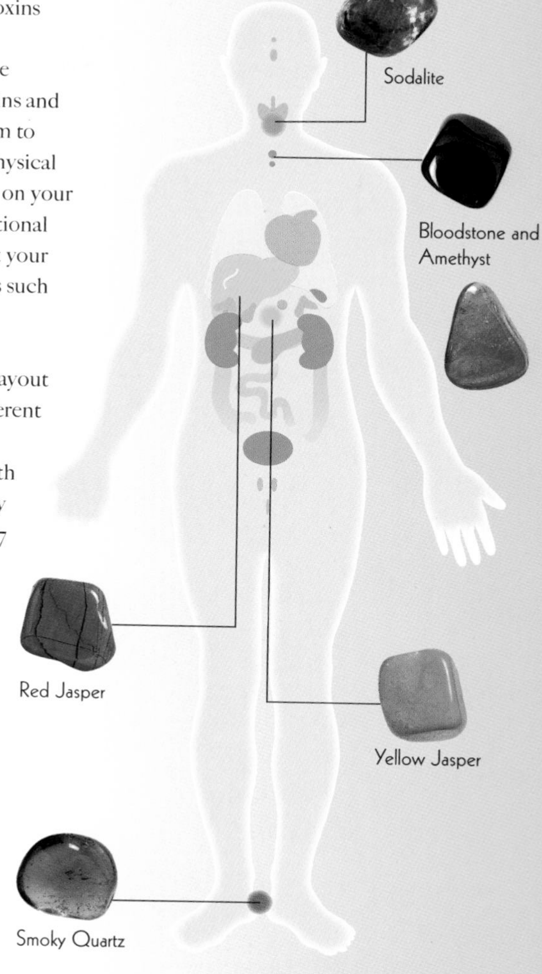

DIRECTORY OF ORGAN AND CRYSTAL CORRESPONDENCES

This list is in no way definitive, and you can add more crystals to it from the crystals that you find effective in the exercises that accompany this chapter.

Bile duct Jasper, Gaspeite, Jade

Bladder and urinary tract Amber, Jasper, Jade, Orange Calcite, Yellow Zincite, Bloodstone

Bowels Jasper, Amber, Ruby, Clear Quartz, Iron Pyrite, Bloodstone

Brain Lapis Lazuli, Fluorite, Magnesite

Endocrine system Amazonite, Amber, Amethyst, Tourmaline, Jasper, Citrine, Fire Agate, Green Quartz, Tanzine Aura Quartz

Eyes Blue Lace Agate, Sapphire, Chrosoprase, Aquamarine, Vivianite

Fallopian tubes and uterus Chrysoprase, Moonstone, Flint

Jasper

Amber

Iron Pyrite

Snakeskin Agate

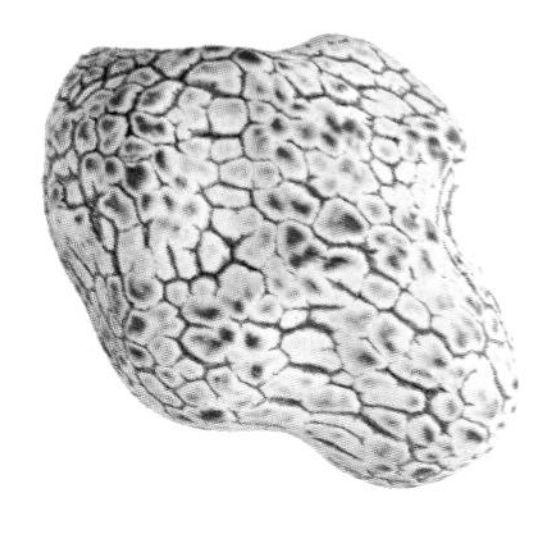

Lapis Lazuli

Gall bladder Carnelian, Gaspeite, Jasper, Topaz, Jade

Liver Amethyst, Tugtupeite, Aquamarine, Beryl, Bloodstone, Charoite, Jasper, Jade, Topaz, Gaspeite

Lungs Rhodochrosite, Chrysocolla, Turquoise, Iron Pyrite

Lymphatic system Tourmaline, Zincite, Halite

Pancreas Pink Opal, Serpentine

Prostate gland Chrysoprase

Skin Snakeskin Agate, Sapphire, Aquamarine

Spleen Green Aventurine, Green Fluorite, Apple Aura Quartz, Green Jade

Stomach Agate, Fire Agate, Turquoise, Lapis Lazuli

Thymus Smithsonite, Bloodstone

Thyroid Tanzine Aura Quartz, Rhodochrostie, Sodalite

Crystals and my mind

Because it secretes mood-altering substances, the brain has a powerful effect on the way we feel. However, you can take control of your mind, and learning to invoke the creativity and clarity of crystal energies helps to reprogram your brain and mind to work to its best advantage.

Crystals can affect how clearly you think and how well you analyse situations. They also calm an overactive mind and invigorate a sluggish one. Keeping a Bloodstone in your pocket during examinations, for instance, helps you to focus and overcomes brain fatigue. Wearing a crystal as earrings or as close as possible to your head or popping one under your pillow at night is another excellent way to keep your mind focused. Crystals that release toxic thoughts or beliefs that no longer serve you or that help you to overcome deeply ingrained patterns of thinking would make effective earrings. You can also use crystal layouts to bring about specific results (see the illustration here and the exercise on page 174).

This exercise is suitable for Any of the crystals mentioned on page 160 or which you choose intuitively.

Work with your crystals now To boost your memory and powers of concentration, turn to Exercise 21: Improving My Mind on page 174.

I'm not quite there yet Read through all your journal entries so far in the exercises within each chapter. Can you spot any ingrained thoughts or beliefs running through your experiences? Do any of the crystals mentioned on page 160 suggest solutions?

Improving my mind layout

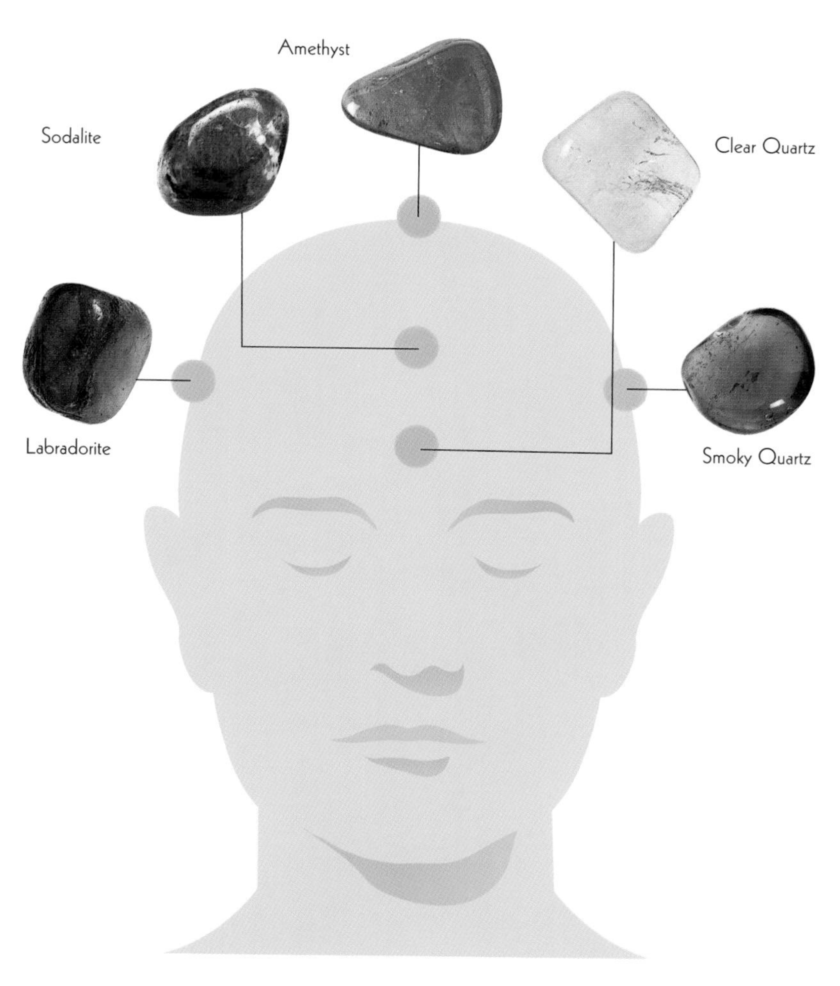

CRYSTALS FOR THE MIND

This is not intended to be a definite list, and you can add crystals as you discover more about their mind-enhancing properties. Make a note of the crystals you find effective in the exercises that accompany this chapter.

Concentration, focus, memory and learning Amethyst, Carnelian, Labradorite, Clear Quartz, Fluorite, Smoky Quartz, Sodalite, Bloodstone

Decision making and lateral thinking Amethyst, Bloodstone, Chrysocolla, Rose Quartz

Creativity Green Aventurine, Jasper, Rose Quartz, Sodalite

Calming mental stress Blue Lace Agate, Celestite

Dissolving rigid mental conditioning Sodalite

Dealing with addictions Amethyst

Overcoming depression Kunzite, Sunstone

Resolving mid-life crises Rose Quartz

Tackling panic attacks Sodalite, Rose Quartz

Dealing with neurosis Green Aventurine

Combatting over-sensitivity Sodalite, Amethyst, Black Tourmaline

Turning negative thoughts to positive ones Smoky Quartz, Sunstone

HEALING EXERCISES

The exercises in this section will help you to keep your mind, immune system, body and emotions in peak condition so that you enjoy well-being and ease.

Crystals for healing myself

Select two or three crystals from the list of immune-system stimulators on page 147 and cleanse them thoroughly (see pages 22–23). You can finger dowse for these or choose them intuitively (see pages 20–21). As an example you might choose Bloodstone because it's a good all-round healing crystal that stimulates or sedates the immune system as required, Fluorite because it's a good viral healer that guards against colds and flu or Sodalite because you're harbouring obsessive, toxic thoughts that are stressing you out as they emerge just before you go to sleep or as you wake up during the night.

Exercise 18 FINDING MY IMMUNE SYSTEM CRYSTAL

AUDIO REFERENCE TRACK 3 (OPTIONAL)

- **You will need:** 2 or 3 cleansed and activated immune-stimulating or other healing crystals (see above)
- **Relax and tune into your thymus** at the centre of your chest, about a hand's breadth down from your collarbone in the same way as you would tune into a crystal (see pages 44–45). Does your thymus feel over-stretched, rapid and racing or does it feel sluggish and slow to react?
- **Consider what might be causing** you stress. If you wish, choose an additional crystal and put it in the appropriate place.
- **Taking each crystal in turn,** place it over your thymus gland. Leave it in place for 10–15 minutes and notice how your body responds. Do you feel more relaxed, does your mind slow down or does a wave of well-being sweep through your body? How does your thymus respond: does it slow down or speed up?

- **Do you become aware** of any other parts of your body needing support – the spleen, for instance, which is an important part of the immune system? If so, find an appropriate crystal, such as Green Aventurine, which protects against psychic vampires who pull on your energy to feed their own.
- **Try tapping the crystal seven times**, either over your thymus or alongside it on both sides. Notice whether this strengthens the effect of the crystal.
- **Once you have established** your favourite immune-stimulating crystal, place it over your thymus and lay a Clear Quartz on the centre of your forehead whenever you would like to stimulate your immune responses. Place your hands in the crease of your groin on both sides. Relax for 10 minutes. (Repeat daily for 1 week.) Alternatively, gently tap the immune-stimulating crystal over your thymus. Now record your experience in the space provided.

My immune-stimulating experience

Date ______________________ **Time** ______________________

Crystals ______________________

My experience ______________________

How did my thymus feel? ______________________

Am I suffering from stress? If so what kind? ______________________

Which immune-stimulating or immune-sedating crystals work best for me?

Does tapping with a crystal work well for me?

What effect did stimulating my immune system for a week have?

Did the quality of my sleep improve?

What are my other major causes of stress and which crystals would help me overcome them?

Releasing myself from the past

This exercise has been designed for use with Rainbow Obsidian, but any banded crystal that you have tuned into will be equally effective. No matter how busy your life is, be sure to allow enough time and space for this journey.

You can either play this journey through from beginning to end and then write up your experience or pause the audio at the musical interludes while you record your experience at each stage.

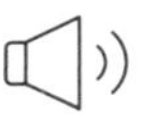

Exercise 19 MY RAINBOW OBSIDIAN JOURNEY

AUDIO REFERENCE TRACK 5 (TO FOLLOW THE SCRIPT, TURN TO PAGES 248–49)

- **You will need:** a cleansed and activated Rainbow Obsidian or other banded crystal
- **Play Track 5 of the audio now** and follow the instructions for the Rainbow Obsidian journey. Then record your experience in the space provided.

My Rainbow Obsidian journey experience

Date ______________________ **Time** ______________________

Crystal ____

My experience ____

Why did I choose this crystal? ______________________________

How was my past affecting my present? ________________________

What did I need to let go?

How easy was it to forgive?

Would another crystal have helped this process?

What gifts did I discover?

How can I put them to work in my life?

What other properties did the crystal have?

My crystal layouts

If you are able to enlist the help of a friend for this exercise, ask him or her to lay the crystals onto you in the order stated. If you have to do the exercise alone, lay the lower stones first at your feet and solar plexus, then lie down and put the others in place. You can adapt this layout to work on other organs and the crystals they correspond with (see pages 156–57). To recap on the site of your organs, see the illustrations on page 153.

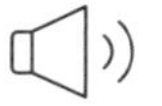

Exercise 20 MY DETOX LAYOUT

AUDIO REFERENCE TRACK 3 (OPTIONAL)

- **You will need**: Bloodstone, Amethyst, Red Jasper, Smoky Quartz, Sodalite, Yellow Jasper or other detoxing stones of your choice
- **Lie down comfortably and relax**. Lay the Bloodstone and Amethyst over your thymus.
- **Lay the Red Jasper over your liver** (at the base of your ribs on your right side).
- **Lay the Smoky Quartz** between your feet.
- **Lay the Sodalite** at the base of your throat.
- **Lay the Yellow Jasper** over your solar plexus. Relax here for 10–20 minutes.
- **Remove the stones and thoroughly cleanse them**. Drink plenty of water over the next 24 hours. Now record your experience in the space provided.

My detox layout experience

Date ______________________ **Time** ______________________

Crystals ______________________

____

My experience ______________________

____

____

____

How I felt before the layout ______________________

____

____

How I felt immediately after the layout ______________________

____

____

How I felt 24 hours later ______________________

____

____

____

Other crystal layout experiences

Date ______________________ **Time** ______________________

Crystals ____

____

Reason for layout ____

____

Immediate effect ____

Effect after 24 hours ____

____

Date ______________________ **Time** ______________________

Crystals ____

____

Reason for layout ____

____

Immediate effect ____

Effect after 24 hours ____

____

Date ______________________ **Time** ______________________

Crystals ____

____

Reason for layout ____

____

Immediate effect ____

____

Effect after 24 hours ____

____

Date ______________________ **Time** ______________________

Crystals ____

____

Reason for layout ____

____

Immediate effect ____

____

Effect after 24 hours ____

____

Crystals for my mind

Crystals can be an enormous support for the mind, and a simple layout can help you to think more clearly and improve your memory. This exercise makes a big mental difference. Before beginning, look back at the map for this simple layout on pages 158–59. You might like to familiarize yourself with the position of the chakras too, shown on pages 84 and 95–96. Repeat the layout every day for a week and vary the stones if you intuitively feel this is appropriate.

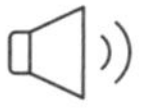

Exercise 21 IMPROVING MY MIND

AUDIO REFERENCE TRACK 3 (OPTIONAL)

- **You will need:** cleansed and activated Amethyst, Sodalite, Clear Quartz, Labradorite and Smoky Quartz tumbled stones
- **Lie down comfortably and place** the Amethyst above your head (at the crown chakra).
- **Place the Sodalite high on your forehead** (over the soma chakra), then place the Clear Quartz lower on your forehead (over the third eye).
- **Place the Labradorite to your right** and the Smoky Quartz to your left.
- **If you have a problem that needs a solution**, think about it for a moment or two and ask for a solution, then forget all about it. Close your eyes and relax with the crystals in place for 10–20 minutes. If you had a problem, let the solution rise into your mind at the appropriate time.
- **Gather up your crystals and stand up slowly**, grounding yourself as you do so by becoming aware of a cord anchoring you to the earth and into your physical body. Now record your experience in the space provided.

My mental improvement experience

Date ______________________ **Time** ______________________

Crystals ______________________

____

____

____

My experience ______________________

____

____

____

____

____

____

How did I feel during the laying of the crystals? ______________________

____

____

____

____

____

Did a solution to my problem become immediately apparent? ______________________

How has my memory been since doing the layout? ______________________

Has repeating the layout for a week improved my concentration? ______________________

HOW DO I KEEP MY CRYSTALS WORKING?

Working with crystals every day

The most important way to keep your crystals working for you is to cleanse, energize and reactivate them regularly. Remember that if you don't ask your crystals to work with you, they will be unsure of their role in your life. The more you work with your crystals, the more your energies will mesh and your stones will pick up an unspoken request in a heartbeat. The best way to ensure this is to talk to and handle your crystals every day. Working with them as often as possible and keeping them around you helps you to live in the crystal world. Respecting your crystals also helps.

Crystals are alive – they have sentience and knowing – and if you honour this and respect their knowledge, they will work even harder for you in return. One of the nicest ways to work daily with your crystals is to put them in your bath (see page 180) or to meditate with them (see page 194). When you are meditating you can create a crystal mandala or focus on one special crystal – once you have done the meditation a few times, your brainwaves will automatically drop into the pattern most conducive for meditation as soon as you pick up your meditation crystal.

This exercise is suitable for Any crystal, but crystal balls or crystals that have planes, flaws and inner landscapes are excellent meditation tools because they provide a focus for your attention and keep your mind busy while your consciousness changes.

Work with your crystal now To meditate with your crystal, turn to Exercise 22: Travelling My Inner Planes on page 194.

I'm not quite there yet Play Track 1 of the audio and follow the instructions for relaxation, focusing and opening.

Crystal bathing

Taking a bath with your crystals is a wonderful experience. Some crystals, such as Halite, dissolve in the water, giving you a thorough energetic cleanse and revitalization. Other crystals give you a crystal love experience.

To create a crystal love bath, prepare the room carefully. Light a rose-scented candle in a Rose Quartz candle holder because rose is the perfume of Venus, the goddess of love. Add a few drops of rose oil to the bathwater if you wish. Spritzing suitable gem essences around the room adds to the ambience, too (see pages 190–92). Use Venus crystals in your bathwater. Rose Quartz is the Goddess of Love's favourite, but Danburite, Larimar, Rhodonite and many other crystals carry her energy.

Either place them in the water or add them as a gem essence. Delicate crystals are best placed around the rim of the bath to avoid damage or disintegration.

When you are in the bath, lie back, close your eyes and let the water gently lap around you, carrying the crystal vibration deep into your skin. Massage around your heart and belly with a crystal. Allow yourself at least 20 minutes and preferably longer to immerse yourself in the crystal vibration, opening your heart to love. As you dry yourself, thank the crystals for their assistance and then carefully dry them.

Rose Quartz

Crystal massage

Crystal wands with gently rounded ends, eggs or tumbled stones make excellent massage wands to gently release tension and infuse you with the qualities of the stone. Use Rose Quartz to give yourself unconditional love and forgiveness, Rhodonite to gently erase memories of abuse, Rutilated Quartz to lift you from a dark mood, Carnelian, Clear Quartz or Red Jasper for all-over revitalization, Amethyst to bring you to a spiritual high, Angelite for an angelic experience, or any other crystal that feels good to you.

Massage the crystal gently over your whole body or as much of it as you can reach. If you have a partner who is willing to massage you with the crystal, so much the better. Sharing the effects of one of your favourite crystals with your lover or friend in this way is a deeply intimate experience, especially if you give massage as well as receive it.

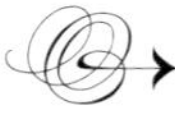

This exercise is suitable for Any rounded or tumbled stone; it is not appropriate to use a pointed crystal for massage.

Work with your crystal now For a soothing crystal massage, turn to Exercise 23: Giving Myself a Crystal Massage on pages 196–97.

I'm not quite there yet Go out and buy yourself a massage wand or crystal egg that really speaks to you.

Rose Quartz – use round end

Amethyst – use round end

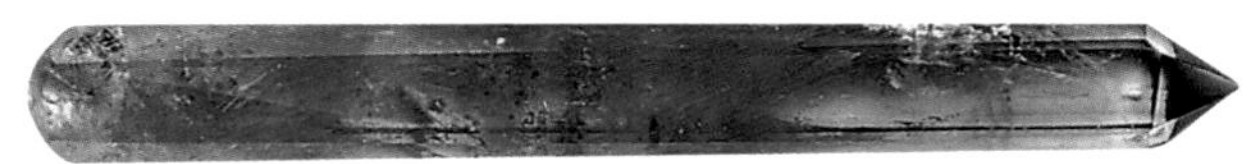

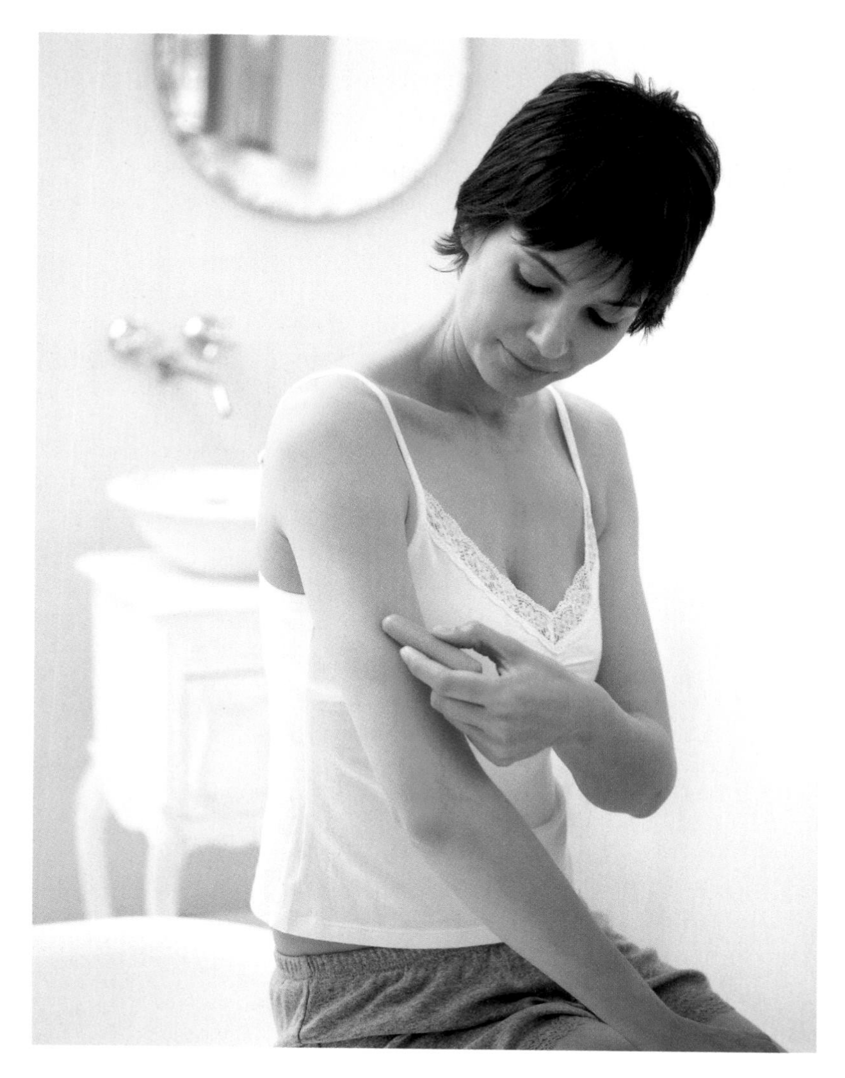

Talking to your crystals

The more you talk to your crystals the more they respond to you – and even though you may laugh at the idea of talking to a crystal, remember that whenever you ask a crystal to work with you, you are talking to it. When you attune to a crystal, you are allowing it to speak to you. This 'talking' can take place out loud or in your mind. Telepathy with a crystal works really well once you have attuned to that specific crystal and has the advantage of pulling in the assistance of the crystal whenever you need it, no matter how far the distance between you. This is particularly powerful if you are in the habit of meditating with your crystals because you can ask the crystal to assist you during your meditation and then forget all about it until you need the crystal input.

You can, of course, carry your crystals with you, either by wearing them or keeping them in your pocket. As you handle them talk to the crystals in your mind. Don't be surprised if they start to talk back to you!

This exercise is suitable for Talking to any of your crystal collection, but this exercise is particularly useful for bi-coloured crystals, such as Merlinite, Zebra Stone, Gaspeite, Atlantasite, Dalmation Stone, Jasper, Rhodonite or crystals that balance yin and yang.

Work with your crystals now To learn to talk to your crystal and find inner balance, turn to Exercise 24: Finding My Inner Balance on pages 198–99. You can apply the principles to any talk you wish to have with your crystals.

I'm not quite there yet Turn back to page 44 and attune yourself to your crystals.

Bi-coloured stones

Graspeite

Atlantasite

Shiva Lingham

Dalmation Stone

Jasper

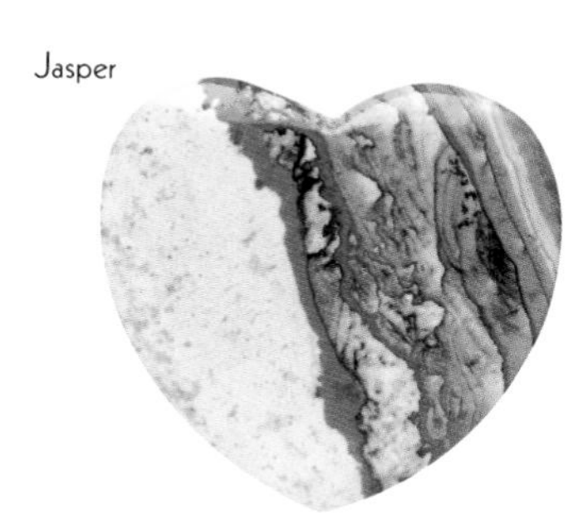

Merlinite

Incorporating new spiritual qualities

The clearer and lighter your own vibrations become, the more closely you can attune yourself with crystals, the more your spiritual gifts will open, and the greater will be the increase in your sensitivity.

Crystals have a deep desire to share the wisdom they have gathered over millions of years in the earth, and they can provide you with spiritual guidance. Much of this guidance comes through dreams and signals, and the more sensitive you are, the more you can become aware of these subtle signs. You can also use the exercise on page 202 to draw specific qualities to yourself, such as compassion, unconditional acceptance and forgiveness or universal love. All you need to do is select the right crystal to bring that quality or spiritual gift to you (see pages 188–89).

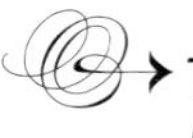

This exercise is suitable for Chrysoprase or Dioptase for compassion; Mangano Calcite, Chrysoberyl, Chrysoprase, Apache Tear, Rhodonite, Infinite Stone, Okenite, Rose Quartz, Rutilated Quartz, Sugilite, Rhodochrosite or Tugtupite for forgiveness; or any other crystal that opens you to spiritual gifts or qualities (see pages 188–89).

Work with your crystals now To open your intuition and spiritual insight, turn to Exercise 25: Accessing My Spiritual Gifts on page 202.

I'm not quite there yet Spend time reading and thinking about the information on pages 188–89.

Spiritual gifts layout

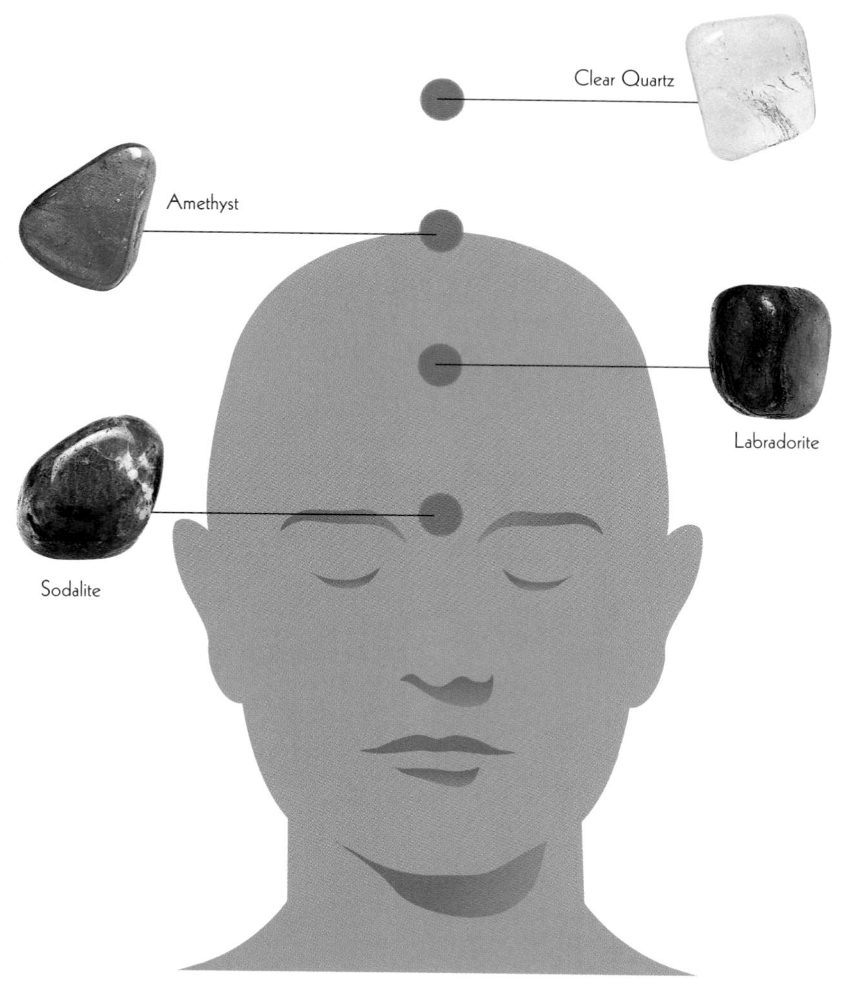

DIRECTORY OF CRYSTALS FOR SPIRITUAL GIFTS

Intuition Knowing things without having to fathom out the reasoning or logic; intuition puts disparate information together and makes a great leap. A subtle sensing takes place in your body or heart, then communicates the information to your mind.
INTUITION-ENHANCING CRYSTALS: Apophyllite, Selenite, Labradorite, Amethyst, Yellow Calcite, Angels Wing Calcite, Lapis Lazuli, Azurite, Moonstone, Star Sapphire, Amazonite, Celestite, Sodalite, Smoky Quartz, Lavender Smithsonite, Azeztulite, Petalite, Phantom Quartz, Ametrine, Aqua Aura, Kyanite, Apatite, Antacamite

---

Inner wisdom Often referred to as the voice of the heart or soul. Attuning to your inner wisdom involves stilling the everyday mind and shutting off stimuli from the outer world. In the silence, you access your own knowing.
WISDOM-RETRIEVING CRYSTALS: Cathedral Quartz, Record Keepers, Lemurian Seed, Phantoms, Elestials, Serpentine, Snow Quartz, Herkimer Diamond, most high-vibration stones

Telepathy Intentionally – and sometimes unintentionally – passing thoughts, words, pictures and symbols from one mind to another without verbalization or visual clues; can operate over vast distances.
TELEPATHY-ENHANCING CRYSTALS: Angelite, Chalcedony, Herkimer Diamond, Selenite, Phantoms, Elestial and other Quartzes

---

Precognition Moving forward in time to access knowledge about the future.
VISION-ENHANCING CRYSTALS: Peridot, Moldavite, Petalite, Azeztulite, Libyan Desert Tecktite, Azurite

---

Retrocognition Moving backward in time to access knowledge about the past, including past-life memories.
VISION-ENHANCING CRYSTALS: Peridot, Moldavite, Petalite, Azeztulite, Libyan Desert Tecktite, Azurite, Variscite, Eudialyte

---

Psychokinesis Moving objects by the power of the mind alone.
PSYCHOKINESIS-ENHANCING CRYSTALS: Quartz, Amber

Remote viewing Also known as astral travelling or journeying. The ability of consciousness to leave the physical body and travel to another place, bringing back a report of what it sees there.
JOURNEYING-ENHANCING CRYSTALS: Shaman Quartz, Phantoms, Avalonite, Brandenberg, Prasiolite, high-vibration stones

---

Clairvoyance Information received through impressions, thoughts, pictures and symbols. Communication is often with another level of existence, such as the spirits of those who have departed, but can involve reading the contents of a sealed envelope and such like.
CLAIRVOYANCE-ENHANCING CRYSTALS: Yellow Labradorite (Bytownite), Quartz, Apophyllite, Azurite with Malachite, high-vibration crystals

---

Clairaudience Information received through a distinct voice – often heard behind the ear – or by an idea 'popping' into the mind.
CLAIRAUDIENCE-ENHANCING CRYSTALS: Dumortierite, Geothite, Orange River Quartz, Phantom Quartz

---

Clairsentience The subtle gift of receiving information from a flower or similar object through sensing.
CLAIRSENTIENCE-ENHANCING CRYSTAL: Preseli Bluestone

Psychometry Ability to read the impressions retained by objects or places.
PSYCHOMETRY-ENHANCING CRYSTAL: Preseli Bluestone

Channelling (trance) A spirit or being who is no longer on earth (or who, it is claimed, is extraterrestrial) who communicates through the medium of a living person using his or her voice box or by passing information into the mind.
CHANNELLING-ENHANCING CRYSTALS: Moldavite, Celestite, Apophyllite, Bustamite, Calcite Fairy Stone, Cavansite, Quantum Quatro, Drusy Quartz, high-vibration crystals

---

Automatic writing When words appear without thought; the feeling that something outside oneself is writing.
WRITING-STIMULATING CRYSTALS: Chinese Writing Stone, Calligraphy Stone

Gem essences

Because crystals work by resonance and vibration, their energy can pass into water – as a gem essence – and then into your body. You can make gem essences from a single crystal or a combination, then add an essence to bathwater, rub it on your skin, disperse it around your aura with your hands, spray it around a room or take a few drops three times a day.

Remember to always use cleansed and activated stones when making essences. Use the indirect method for toxic or friable stones. These include Malachite, Galena, Stibnite, Tiffany Stone, Bornite, Beryllium, Halite, Selenite and all fragile crystals. If you are unsure whether a crystal is toxic or friable, use a tumbled crystal and the indirect method.

Making a gem mother essence: direct method

First ascertain whether the crystal is toxic (see above; if you suspect it might be toxic, use the indirect method described on page 192). Then cleanse your crystal (see pages 22–23).

Place the cleansed crystal in a clean glass bowl and cover with pure spring water. Place the bowl in the sunlight for up to 12 hours (cover if necessary). Some essences enjoy being out in the moonlight or during a rain storm. Remove the crystal from the water.

If the essence is to be stored for more than two days, pour the water into a clean glass bottle until one-third full. Make a mixture of two-thirds brandy or vodka and one-third spring water and use to top up the bottle. Clearly label the bottle with the name of the essence and date. This is a mother essence or tincture. Store in a cool, dark place and dilute before use by adding 7 drops to a bottle of one-third brandy to two-thirds water. This is a stock bottle. Dilute again with 7 drops to one-third brandy and two-thirds spring water (see page 204).

Note Do not take toxic crystal essences by mouth.

Making a gem mother essence: indirect method

Cleanse your crystal (see pages 22–23). Place the cleansed crystal in a small, clean glass bowl and stand this bowl in a larger bowl.

Pour pure spring water into the outer bowl only. Place the bowls in sunlight for up to 12 hours (cover if necessary).

Remove the water from the outer bowl and follow the instructions for the direct method on page 190.

This exercise is suitable for Any crystal but check whether it is toxic or fragile before making the essence and, if so, use the indirect method (see above). To make a protection essence, use Black Tourmaline, Smoky Quartz, Green Aventurine or other protective stones that remove negativity.

Work with your crystals now To make a healing gem essence, turn to Exercise 26: Using My Gem Essence on page 204.

I'm not quite there yet Turn back to pages 146–60 to check out the healing properties of the crystals you are considering using to make a gem essence.

EXERCISES TO KEEP CRYSTALS WORKING

These exercises will help you to deepen your connection with your crystals, raise your spiritual awareness and open your intuition further. They will also help you to incorporate new qualities into your spiritual development and to try out gem essences.

Meditating with crystals

Before starting crystal meditation, make sure that you will not be disturbed, turn off your phone and dim the lights. You can sit in any position you find comfortable. Remember to cleanse your crystal before use (see pages 22–23).

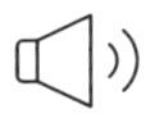

Exercise 22 TRAVELLING MY INNER PLANES

AUDIO REFERENCE TRACK 3 (OPTIONAL)

- **You will need:** a cleansed and activated crystal ball or a crystal with inner planes, flaws, phantoms or a landscape
- **Sit comfortably and hold your crystal or ball** loosely in your hands or place it on a table in front of you with your hands resting on it. Relax and let your eyes go slightly out of focus. Breathe gently into your belly so that you establish a natural, slow rhythm.
- **Let your eyes softly follow** the inner planes of your crystal or ball, journeying all around the crystal until you feel calm, peaceful and centred.
- **When you are ready, close your eyes** and allow that peace to take you deep into yourself to a place of absolute stillness and silence.
- **Again, when you are ready,** bring your attention back out to the ball or crystal. Open your eyes, look at the crystal and thank it for its assistance. Take your hands away from the ball, disconnecting from the crystal energy.
- **Feel your feet placed firmly** on the floor and your sitting bones on the chair. Visualize a crystal bubble extending all around you, protecting your aura. Stand up and stretch. Now record your experience in the space provided.

My inner plane experience

Date ______________________ **Time** ______________________

Crystal ______________________

My experience ______________________

Experiencing a crystal massage

Crystal massage is a very gentle experience and one that allows you to really feel the energy of the crystal and the love it has for you. Choose your crystal in accordance with what you wish to receive from the massage (see the Crystal Directory on pages 26–32) and remember to cleanse and activate the crystal before you start (see pages 22–23). The most potent time to practise this exercise is at the full moon or the dark of the moon.

Exercise 23 GIVING MYSELF A CRYSTAL MASSAGE

AUDIO REFERENCE TRACK 3 (OPTIONAL)

- **You will need**: a cleansed and activated crystal massage wand or tumbled stone
- **Lie in a warm place** where you will not be disturbed. You can either massage over your clothes or onto your skin, whichever feels more comfortable.
- **When you are comfortably settled**, repeat the feeling-safe affirmation to yourself three times: 'I am safe, I am loved, I trust myself and my crystal.'
- **Take your crystal** and hold it in your hands, asking that it helps you to relax and heal (or whatever else you want from the massage). Feel the loving energy of the crystal warming your hands and passing through your body.
- **When you feel ready**, gently stroke the crystal all over your body; you may like to begin with your hands or feet. Use circular massage movements or sweeping strokes, whichever feel more comfortable and pleasurable.
- **Use the crystal to explore your body fully**. Take your time. Notice which areas feel least comfortable, lay the crystal gently there and allow the healing energies of the crystal to make this part of your body feel good.

- **Keep stroking and massaging** your body with the crystal until your whole body is glowing with the pleasure of crystal love.
- **When you are ready** to end the massage, lie quietly for five minutes and then get up slowly. Have a good stretch and move around or simply go to sleep with your massage crystal beneath your pillow. Don't forget to record your thoughts in the space provided.

My crystal massage experience

Date ______________________ **Time** ______________________

Crystal ______________________

My experience ______________________

Listening to your crystals

The following exercise helps your crystal to speak back to you! Do not use music for this exercise: you need to be fully aware of your crystal speaking. All of us have a balance of masculine and feminine energy within us, and this exercise helps you to find equilibrium.

Choose a bi-coloured crystal that has as equal a balance of the two colours as possible. The Shiva Lingham on page 185 is somewhat more feminine than masculine, for instance, but is highly suitable for feminine working since its masculine shape brings balance.

Exercise 24 FINDING MY INNER BALANCE

- **You will need:** a cleansed and activated bi-coloured crystal, such as a Shiva Lingham (see page 185).
- **Holding your Shiva Lingham** in both hands, ask it to help you find inner balance.
- **Taking your Shiva Lingham** in your left hand, place the lighter coloured part on the left side of your body, wherever feels intuitively right (you can move it around if you wish). You may wish to start with your head and then work down your body.
- **Ask the Shiva Lingham** to tell you how your feminine energy works, how receptive, nurturing and giving you are, and how you use your powers of assertion. If you are working down your body, you can ask at the mental level (your head), at the emotional level (your heart and solar plexus) and at the active level (your belly).
- **Listen for the answer** in your heart or slightly behind your physical ear, where your inner ear lies.

- **Now place the darker end** of the Shiva Lingham wherever feels comfortable on the right side of your body. Ask the crystal to tell you how you use your masculine energy, how assertive and active you are and how much you initiate and protect. Listen for the answer as before.
- **Finally, take the Shiva Lingham** in both hands and place it on the mid-line of your body – you may want to move through each major chakra in turn, starting at your belly (see pages 84–85).
- **Ask the crystal to help you** find a point of balance between your masculine and feminine energy. When you reach that point of balance, rest quietly in its stillness.
- **Then ask your crystal to speak**. Don't forget to record your experience in the space provided.

My finding balance experience

Date ______________________ **Time** ______________________

Crystal ______________________

My experience ______________________

How easy was it to hear my crystal speak? ______________________

Was my feminine or masculine energy stronger? ______________________

Do I think in a masculine or feminine way?

Do I assert myself in a masculine or feminine way?

How did it feel to reach a point of balance?

What did my crystal say in the silence?

Incorporating new spiritual qualities

This exercise helps you to open your intuition and access other spiritual gifts. It is a useful meditation that slowly opens your third eye and enhances your ability to see beyond the everyday. Once you have done the layout shown on page 187, vary the crystals to see which opens your third eye most easily. You can vary the exercise by replacing the Labradorite with Bytownite or Spectrolite (higher resonances of the basic crystal) or with an Apophyllite pyramid or other intuition-enhancing crystal (see page 188). You can also use crystals to help you journey out of your body, to open clairvoyance or to assimilate spiritual qualities into your life (see page 188–89).

Exercise 25 ACCESSING MY SPIRITUAL GIFTS

AUDIO REFERENCE TRACK 3 (OPTIONAL)

- **You will need**: cleansed and activated Clear Quartz, Amethyst, Labradorite, Sodalite or other intuition-enhancing crystals
- **Lie down comfortably** and place the Clear Quartz above your head.
- **Place the Amethyst** so that it is just touching the crown of your head. Place the Labradorite at the top of your forehead and Sodalite between your eyebrows.
- **Close your eyes** and take your attention to your third eye. Leave the crystals in place for 15 minutes and note the effect on your third eye and your intuition.
- **When you have finished** gather up the crystals, stand up and ground yourself firmly by becoming aware of a grounding cord anchoring you to the earth and into your physical body. Picture shutters closing over your third eye to protect it.

My intuition-opening experience

Date ______________________ **Time** ______________________

Crystals ______________________

____

My experience ______________________

____

____

____

Other crystals I tried ______________________

____

Effect ______________________

____

____

____

____

How is my intuition working now? ______________________

____

____

____

Healing with gem essences

Before starting this exercise, ask yourself for what healing purpose you would like to make a gem essence. Do you want to bring balance to your physical body, your mind or your emotions, or do you have a more spiritual goal? Perhaps you would like to use the essence as a room protection spray. When you have decided on your purpose, select the appropriate crystal or crystals from pages 146–60, cleanse and activate them (see pages 22–23), and then make the mother essence following the direct or indirect method on pages 190–92.

Exercise 26 USING MY GEM ESSENCE

- **You will need**: mother essence (made from cleansed crystal(s), clean glass bowl, spring water), small dropper bottles, brandy or vodka, spring water
- **Make a dosage bottle**: take 7 drops of the mother essence and place into a small dropper bottle. Top up with one-third brandy or vodka to two-thirds spring water. This is a stock bottle, and it will keep for several weeks in a cool, dark place. Clearly label and date it.
- **Make a dosage or spray bottle**: take a further 7 drops from the stock bottle and add them to a new bottle. Top up with one-third brandy or vodka to two-thirds spring water. (If making a spray for immediate use, omit the brandy.)
- **To use the essence**, finger dowse (see page 21) to ask whether you should take the essence under your tongue (7 drops), over a chakra or affected organ, or disperse it into your aura, your environment or your bathwater. Use the essence three times a day as directed for at least a week and preferably longer, recording your experience in the spaces provided.

My gem essence experience

Date essence made ______________________ **Date** ______________________

Crystal(s) ______________________

Purpose ______________________

____

____

Effect ______________________

____

____

Date essence made ______________________ **Date** ______________________

Crystal(s) ______________________

Purpose ______________________

____

____

Effect ______________________

____

____

Date essence made ______________________ **Date** ______________________

Crystal(s) ____

Purpose ____

____

____

Effect ____

____

____

____

Date essence made ______________________ **Date** ______________________

Crystal(s) ____

Purpose ____

____

____

Effect ____

____

____

____

Date essence made ______________________ **Date** ______________________

Crystal(s) ______________________

Purpose ______________________

____

____

Effect ______________________

____

____

____

Date essence made ______________________ **Date** ______________________

Crystal(s) ______________________

Purpose ______________________

____

____

Effect ______________________

____

____

____

Date essence made ______________ **Date** ______________

Crystal(s) ______________

Purpose ______________

____

____

Effect ______________

____

____

____

Date essence made ______________ **Date** ______________

Crystal(s) ______________

Purpose ______________

____

____

Effect ______________

____

____

____

TAKING CRYSTAL WORK FURTHER

Working with higher vibration crystals

High-vibration crystals have a finer, lighter and more refined vibration than the crystals used so far in this book. Their energy connects both to higher dimensional realities and to your core spiritual identity, bringing about multi-dimensional healing and spiritual alchemy. These crystals stimulate new chakras now coming on-line, such as the soul star and stellar gateway (see pages 92–96), while working with the traditional chakras to accommodate their high-frequency energies. Most high-vibration stones work slowly to bring about physical change because they act on the subtle levels of being first and are more suitable for multi-dimensional work.

Having one of these 'high vibes' stones in your collection could be extremely beneficial if you are consciously working to embody spiritual energies, raise your vibrations and activate your lightbody or open the higher chakras. Some of these stones are unique, 'one-off' crystals, such as Tugtupite or Tanzanite (a member of the Zoisite family), some are a coloured variation of a basic crystal like Rainbow Moonstone or Paraiba Tourmaline, but others may be a specific form of Quartz, such as Azeztulite, or Quartz that has been alchemically enhanced, such as the Aura Quartzes.

Note You should only begin to work with a high-vibration crystal when your vibrations are in harmony with the crystal. It is important to have completed your healing and evolutionary work in this earth dimension first and to have worked through all the previous exercises in this book.

This exercise is suitable for Rainbow and Blue Moonstone, Selenite, Azeztulite, Petalite, Danburite, Golden and Aqua Aura Danburite, Paraiba Tourmaline, Tanzanite, Natrolite, Mystic Topaz, Ajoite, Beryllonite, Stellar Beam Calcite, Purple Scapolite, Tugtupite, Greenlandite, Brandenberg Amethyst, Spectrolite, Herderite, Tanzine and other Aura Quartzes, Vera Cruz Amethyst and Super 7, Elestial, Lemurian, Sichuan, Celestial, Spirit, Indicolite, Nirvana, Satyalokan and Sayamani Quartz or other high-vibration crystals.

Work with your crystal now To compare high- and low-vibration crystals turn to Exercise 27: Comparing My High- and Low-vibration Crystals on page 226. Then to attune yourself to these crystals turn to Exercise 28: Attuning to My High-vibration Crystals on page 228.

I'm not quite there yet Turn to pages 92–96 to find out more about opening your higher chakras or to enhance your ability to feel crystal energies turn to page 44.

Tanzine Aura Quartz

Paraiba Tourmaline

Tugtupeite

HIGH-VIBRATION CRYSTAL DIRECTORY

This directory is not a definitive guide, and there are other high-vibration crystals that you might like to work with (see *The Crystal Bible* volume 2). Write your experiences in the spaces on pages 229–31 as you discover them.

Brandenberg

Brandenberg (trigonal; clear, amethyst, smoky) In my opinion, the crystal that has everything, Brandenberg connects to the perfect blueprint that has been there since before time began. Excellent for all inter-dimensional work and for accessing high vibrations, opening all the new chakras.

Pink Danburite

Danburite (orthorhombic; pink, lilac or golden) The perfect heart-healer, Danburite can transport you to higher dimensions to connect to your higher self and angelic guidance, especially in its golden form. It assists with karmic healing, equipping you to break away from the past and follow your soul path. Facilitates emotional detoxification on all levels.

Celestite

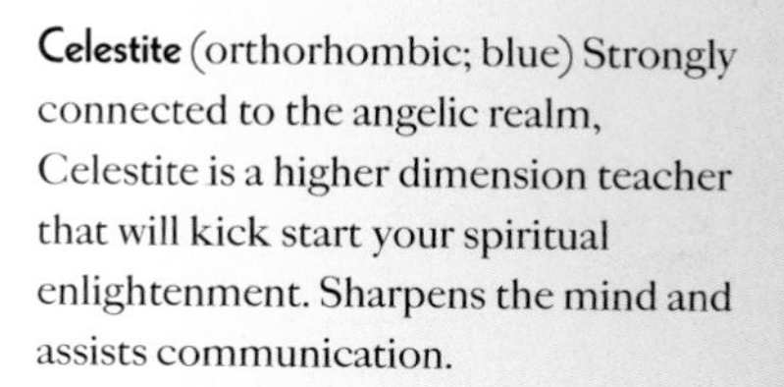
Celestite (orthorhombic; blue) Strongly connected to the angelic realm, Celestite is a higher dimension teacher that will kick start your spiritual enlightenment. Sharpens the mind and assists communication.

Labradorite/Bytownite/Spectrolite/ Hypersthene (triclinic; blue-green-grey, yellow, lilac) Perfect for separating your energy from that of another person and deflecting psychic attack. Labradorite is an excellent protector for the aura.

Bytownite, Spectrolite and Hypersthene are more refined vibrations of this mystical crystal. They open psychic gifts and higher chakras and ground spiritual insights.

Spectrolite

Tanzanite (orthorhombic; purple) An excellent journeying tool, Tanzanite facilitates altered states of consciousness and is an ascension crystal. Assists in multi-dimensional cellular and karmic healing and helps you to find your vocation.

Tanzanite

Azeztulite (trigonal; white, colourless, golden-yellow) A light-bearer, Azeztulite works at the spiritual level, creating chakra connections to higher reality and expanding consciousness. It facilitates a vibrational shift by bringing higher frequencies to earth and raising your personal vibration. You then give out a higher vibration. Begin with the opaque crystal and move onto the clear and golden when your energies have adjusted.

Azeztulite

Lemurian (trigonal; clear white, smoky, pink, golden, green, blue) Excellent for karmic and chakra cleansing, it opens new channels in the subtle and physical bodies. Assist in remembering our spiritual selves with All That Is. Grid for angelic contact, energy portals and regaining inherent abilities.

Lemurian

Paraiba Tourmaline (trigonal; turquoise) A new find, Paraiba is an enhanced Tourmaline with radiant heart energy that connects to the angels of truth and wisdom. Carries infinite compassion and encourages service to the planet and humanity. Calms over-reactions of the immune system and auto-immune diseases.

Paraiba Tourmaline

Moldavite

Moldavite (non-crystalline meteorite; deep olive green) Offers awareness of cause and source of dis-ease and supports healing, identifying the gift within illness and potentials. Aligns the chakras, integrates the divine blueprint and accelerates spiritual growth. Brings you into communication with your higher self and cosmic messengers.

Phenacite

Phenacite (trigonal; white, clear, pink) Purifies and raises consciousness to a high frequency, bringing cosmic information to earth. It heals the soul and prepares subtle and physical bodies as a vehicle for the activated lightbody. Energies are available to those who have shifted their personal vibration to a higher level. Amplifies the energy of other healing crystals.

Spirit Quartz

Spirit Quartz (trigonal; white, smoky, 'citrine') Provides insights into family problems, tightly focusing healing that reaches multi-dimensions. It promotes self-forgiveness and reprogrammes cellular memory. Spirit Quartz takes you to meet the spirits of your ancestors and can be programmed for ancestral healing, and reframing the past. An excellent stone to accompany the dying.

Selenite (monoclinic; white) Existing at the interface between spirit and matter, Selenite is crystallized divine light and anchors the lightbody in incarnation. Helpful for ascertaining your soul purpose and when you are still working on lessons. It is water soluble.

Polished Selenite

Petalite (monoclinic; white, pink) Assisting in spiritual purification and ancestral healing, Petalite is a shamanic crystal. Ideal for guiding a vision quest and for aligning the aura and opening the higher crown chakras.

Petalite

Tugtupite (tetragonal; pink, white, grey) Although exceedingly rare and expensive, Tugtupite is one of the most valuable crystals for heart-healing and awakening the heart-seed chakra (below the breastbone). It unites a compassionate heart with an illumined mind, bringing infinite peace. Useful for defending your liver against other people's anger. It promotes forgiveness and the ability to give of oneself in service.

Tugtupite

Satyamani Quartz

Satyamani/Satyaloka Quartz (trigonal; clear, white, yellow, grey) Specially prepared by monks in the Himalayas to bring the flame of pure consciousness to earth and to facilitate a vibrational shift in healing, these Quartzes infuse the body with transformational energy. When placed on the soma chakra they activate the light- body and on the third eye the illumined mind. Combines well with Nirvana Quartz.

Purple Nirvana Quartz

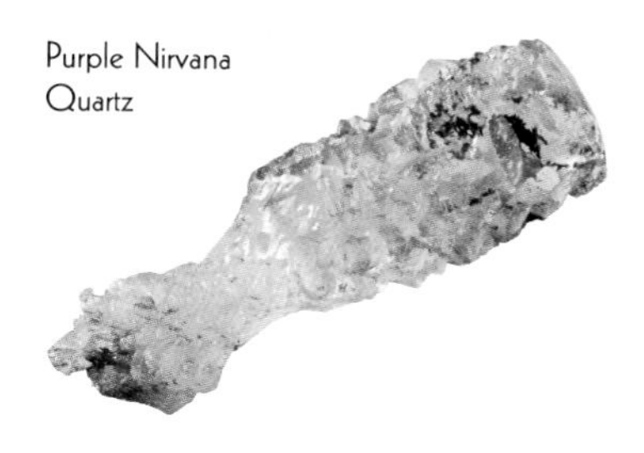

Nivrvana Quartz (trigonal; white, pink, purple) Another of the Himalayan Quartzes, Nirvana Quartz is a crystal for spiritual alchemy and enlightenment. It holds crystallized divine consciousness and facilitates a profound shift in awareness, helping the soul to shed its karmic load. Excellent for opening the soul star chakra.

Blue Moonstone

Blue Moonstone (monoclinic; blue on white) One of the most powerfully activating stones for unawakened spiritual potential, Blue Moonstone prepares the physical body for the incorporation of the lightbody and reaches extremely high levels of consciousness. Place on the back of the neck to release muscle tension and allow subtle energies to flow through this area.

Crystal rituals and journeys

Rituals are a way of drawing something into your life. Whether you require abundance, assistance or love, all you need do is choose the right crystals and carry out the rituals respectfully with focused attention and intention. Journeys offer another powerful way to work with crystals, and this chapter's exercises end with a journey into the unconditional love and acceptance of All That Is (see pages 336–38).

Amethyst geode

Although undertaking a ritual or journey is a serious matter that demands focus and intention, rituals and journeys also take you into a bright and joyful, almost playful, connection with your crystal companions. It is as if the crystal enjoys the experience as much as you do.

Timing rituals

Planning the timing can make an immense difference to the success of a ritual. If you want to draw something into your life, perform your ritual under the light of the new moon and continue until full moon, and if you want to send something out into the world, perform it at full moon time and continue until new moon.

Preparing the room

Rituals are best carried out in a prepared space (see pages 124–28). It is also traditional to bathe and put on clean clothes before performing a ritual and to work in candlelight. If you are journeying or carrying out a ritual or journey, make sure that phones are turned off and you will not be disturbed.

Attracting love

Crystals are just waiting to bring more love into your life, and nothing is more effective at attracting love than Rose Quartz. Place a big chunk of this beautiful crystal, activated to bring an abundance of love, in the relationship corner of your home (the far right corner from the door). Alternatively, place it by your bed, asking it to attract exactly the right partner for you – you won't have to wait long! Indeed, one woman found the effect so powerful that she had to cool it down with a gentle Amethyst to bring in one potential lover at a time and to enable her to choose the right man.

Using affirmations

Making an affirmation while holding a crystal is a powerful ritual in itself that takes only a few moments of your time. This ritual requires total focus and intention while you carry it out, and the more emotion you can put into an affirmation, the stronger it will be. To make a love affirmation, for example, hold a piece of Rose Quartz or Danburite and repeat the following words several times a day. It is important that you phrase the affirmation in the present tense to bring it into manifestation – 'I attract love into my life, my life is full of love right now, my life is full of abundant love, I am a magnet for love' – and then let it go.

Rose Quartz

Attracting love

Carrying out rituals with crystals to attract or re-energize love can be highly potent. The love ritual on pages 232–33 uses romantic Rose Quartz, which is surprisingly powerful for such a gentle crystal. This becomes less surprising perhaps when you learn that pink – and Rose Quartz – is associated with Venus, the goddess of love and desire. Amorous Venus rules passion and eroticism, love and affection, and so Rose Quartz attracts a love that is tender and passionate, erotic and exciting. Adding Danburite to Rose Quartz emphasizes the unconditional, mutually supportive twin-flame aspect of love. This crystal packs a powerful punch into a small space. If you desire loving, supportive companionship, you could replace the Danburite with Sugilite. And if it's a hot date you are after, replace Danburite with lusty Ruby or fiery Garnet, powerful attractors of erotic love. Green Aventurine invites passion into the lives of those of more mature years.

When you are intending to perform a love ritual, try wearing pink or red, depending on whether you want to attract romance or red-hot passion. If you wish, you can also burn a sweetgrass smudge or rose incense to prepare the room, and anoint yourself with rose oil. Pink candles will set the scene and the right background music will assist your concentration – try playing Track 3 on the audio. When you are carrying out a love ritual, consciously make your movements slow and sensuous and move with voluptuous intent.

With imagination and the right stones you can adapt the love ritual on page 232–33 for other purposes: for an abundance ritual, use Grossular Garnet, Citrine, Carnelian, Green Aventurine, in a Star of David grid (see page 128); to call in assistance, use Selenite, Celestite or any of the angelic-attuned stones; and to connect to All That Is, use an Amethyst or other crystal geode.

This ritual is suitable for Rose Quartz, Danburite or any of the heart crystals your intuition chooses; try Rhodochrosite, Pink Crackle Quartz, Tugtupeite, Almandine Garnet, Kunzite, Larimar, Sugilite, Pink Tourmaline, Topaz, Ruby or Garnet; alternatively try Green Aventurine (for love in later life) or Red Carnelian (to revitalize existing love).

Work with your crystals now Use your intuition to choose a suitable crystal (see pages 20–21), then for a ritual to attract love into your life turn to Exercise 29: My Attracting Love Ritual on pages 232–33, or for a journey to connect with All That Is, turn to Exercise 30: My Wholeness Meditation on pages 236–37.

I'm not quite there yet Ask yourself why you are not ready to call love into your life. You may have a perfectly valid reason that makes this ritual inappropriate at this time or you may need to do more work on self-development to open your heart to receive love (see pages 218–20).

EXERCISES TO TAKE CRYSTAL WORK FURTHER

These exercises will help you to attune to higher vibration crystals and to carry out rituals or journeys and meditations. They will increase your capacity to attract and give out love and to connect with All That Is in harmony with your crystal companions.

Exploring high-vibration crystals

Practise this exercise to feel the difference between higher and lower vibration crystals. It is suitable for use with crystals such as an ordinary clear Quartz point and one of the high-vibration Quartzes such as a Brandenberg, or with an ordinary Moonstone and a Rainbow or Blue Moonstone (which have progressively higher frequencies). Some of the higher vibration crystals are a more refined form of a crystal that already has a high vibration: Spectrolite is a higher resonance of Labradorite, for instance, although Labradorite is itself a high-vibration crystal.

Exercise 27 COMPARING MY HIGH- AND LOW-VIBRATION CRYSTALS

AUDIO REFERENCE TRACK 3 (OPTIONAL)

- **You will need**: pairs of cleansed and activated higher and lower vibration crystals (see above)
- **Place the pairs of crystals** on a table in front of you, well spaced out. Put your receptive hand first over the lower vibration crystal and attune to its energy.
- **Now put your receptive hand over** the higher vibration crystal until you can attune to its energy. Notice the difference between the two crystals and how this one affects your body and the subtle energy field around you. Note whether this crystal takes you to a higher dimension or opens a higher chakra.
- **Repeat the exercise** with another pair of crystals. Do this until you have worked with each of the pairs. Try changing hands to feel the difference.

My high- and low-vibration crystal experience

Date ______________________ **Time** ______________________

Pair of crystals ______________________

My experience ______________________

____

What I noticed about the lower vibration crystal ______________________

____

What I noticed about the higher vibration crystal ______________________

____

Date ______________________ **Time** ______________________

Pair of crystals ______________________

My experience ______________________

____

What I noticed about the lower vibration crystal ______________________

____

What I noticed about the higher vibration crystal ______________________

____

Working with high-vibration crystals

Not every high-vibration crystal will resonate with you, and the key to succesful working with crystals is to find the ones to which you can attune. If the crystal provokes a healing challenge, remove it and hold a Smoky or Chlorite Quartz between your feet to stabilize your energies. Return to the crystal when you have completed your healing or choose another.

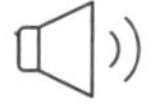

Exercise 28 ATTUNING TO MY HIGH-VIBRATION CRYSTALS

AUDIO REFERENCE TRACK 2 (TO FOLLOW THE SCRIPT, TURN TO PAGES 244–45)

- **You will need:** various cleansed and activated high-vibration crystals (see the High-vibration Crystal Directory on pages 212–17)
- **Hold a high-vibration crystal gently** and sit quietly listening to track 2 on the audio. Your body may vibrate as it attunes to the crystal or you may be instantly transported to another energetic dimension; both reactions show that this crystal will work with you. If this does not happen, choose another crystal to work with, and try this one later when your vibrations have shifted.
- **Once you have established contact** with a crystal, lie down and place it on your higher chakras (see pages 92–93) to see what effect that has. If appropriate, allow the crystal to open these chakras. Ask the crystal to introduce its energetic capabilities to you and to show you how to work with it for best results. Remember to record any additional properties you discover about the crystal.
- **Repeat the exercise** with another high-vibration crystal when appropriate. Don't forget to record your observations in the space provided.

My high-vibration attuning experience

Date ______________________ **Time** ______________________

Crystal ____

My experience ____

____

____

____

____

____

Date ______________________ **Time** ______________________

Crystal ____

My experience ____

____

____

____

____

____

Date ______________________ Time ______________________

Crystal ______________________

My experience ______________________

Date ______________________ Time ______________________

Crystal ______________________

My experience ______________________

Date ______________________ **Time** ______________________

Crystal ____

My experience ____

____

____

____

____

____

____

Date ______________________ **Time** ______________________

Crystal ____

My experience ____

____

____

____

____

____

____

Calling-in love ceremony

This attracting love ritual is a powerful one; do it with unconditional love and compassion for yourself and with the intention of attracting toward you the most perfect love imaginable. If you already have a lover, rather than calling in your twin-flame in the ritual, ask that more love manifests between you and your lover and that the relationship becomes the best it can possibly be. The most potent time to practise this ritual is at the new moon.

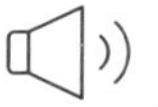

Exercise 29 MY ATTRACTING LOVE RITUAL

AUDIO REFERENCE TRACK 3 (OPTIONAL)

- **You will need**: 4 cleansed and activated Rose Quartz and Danburite crystals, 4 pink candles in 4 Rose Quartz holders, silk cloth
- **Place the crystals and candles** on a table covered with the silk cloth. Position one candle to the north, welcoming in love from that direction as you light it. Place the others to the south, east and west, again welcoming love from each direction as you light the candles.
- **Take your Rose Quartz crystals** into your hands and sit facing the table (if the crystals are large, hold one at a time or place your hands over them). Close your eyes and quietly attune to the crystals.
- **Let the energy of the crystals flow** through your hands, up your arms and into your heart. As the energy reaches your heart, feel it open out and expand. Touch the crystals to your heart. Rose Quartz is a powerful heart cleanser and healer, so allow your heart to be purified by the energies of the crystals. Say, out loud: 'I am a magnet for love. I welcome love into my heart and love into my life.' Place the crystals back on the table in the appropriate place.

- **Pick up the Danburite**. Say out loud, 'I call on my twin-flame to be present and to manifest fully and lovingly in my life' or, 'I call on the love between my lover and myself to manifest fully and unconditionally, loving and supporting us both'.
- **Sit quietly for a few moments** with your eyes focused on the crystals. Picture how life will be when you have the deeply passionate and mutually supportive love of your twin-flame at your side, or when you and your lover manifest all the love that is possible between you. Send that picture out into the future, unrolling it before you so that you walk that path with love.
- **When you are ready** to complete the ritual, get up and blow out each candle in turn saying: 'I send light and love into the world and it returns to me tenfold.' Either leave the crystals on the table or place them around your bed. Don't forget to record your experience in the space provided.

My attracting love experience

Date ______________________ **Time** ______________________

Crystals ______________________

My experience ______________________

The result of my experience ______________________________

Was anything standing in the way of me accepting love? ______________

Connecting to All That Is

This is one of my favourite meditations. I have practised it for more than 35 years and never tire of it. The cave always expands and takes me to a new part of myself and All That Is. Give yourself plenty of time to practise this exercise and make sure that you will not be disturbed. If you have a big Amethyst geode that is too large for you to hold, place it on a table in front of you. You can expand on the exercise on future occasions by checking out whether there are any areas of the cave you have not visited, especially at the higher levels. Look out for hidden doorways and narrow tunnels. Explore whatever you find there, asking for a light to show you the way.

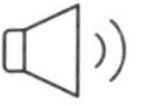

Exercise 30 MY WHOLENESS MEDITATION

AUDIO REFERENCE TRACK 3 (OPTIONAL)

- **You will need**: a cleansed and activated Amethyst geode (see page 218).
- **Sit comfortably and look carefully** at your Amethyst geode. When you can remember its contours, close your eyes. Without opening your eyes, look up to the point above and between your eyebrows, your 'third eye'. Feel this eye open. Breathe gently and withdraw your attention from the outside world, focusing it deep inside yourself.
- **Hold your Amethyst** in whichever hand feels comfortable or place your hands on it and be aware of its vibrations radiating up your arm and into your third eye at the centre of your forehead; feel its energy opening and expanding your inner awareness.

- **Now picture yourself standing** on the bank of a wide river that is flowing gently to the sea. Upstream in the far distance you can see high blue mountains and, at their foot, a shining lake. In front of you is a small wooden jetty with a boat tied up beside it. A boatman is waiting to help you into the boat.
- **Settle yourself comfortably** in the boat and visualize the boatman casting the boat off and guiding it upstream, moving quickly against the current. You can see the banks passing by and soon the river opens out into a beautiful lake. As you cross the lake, you can see a narrow river is coming down from the mountains and flowing into the lake. The boatman takes you as far up this river as it is possible to go. He ties up the boat and helps you out onto a rocky ledge.
- **Follow this ledge up into the mountains**; as it twists and turns you can see light shining in front of you until you enter a crystal cave. The cave is a huge Amethyst geode, light flickering from its every point.
- **Find a comfortable place to settle yourself** and allow yourself to merge with the energy of the Amethyst, enfolded within the geode. Let your spirit become one with the infinity of being. Ask the Amethyst to show you your soul path.
- **When you have found your soul path**, ask to be shown the guides and helpers who surround you in the unseen world. Ask them how they can help you and set out any specific requests you have for assistance.
- **Now let your spirit become one** with the infinity of being. Become aware of how ancient the crystal is, how it is light personified and how it is the divine taking on form. Then let your spirit become one with the infinity of being. Let go. Expand into All That Is. Simply merge and be.

- **When you are ready to leave** the crystal cave, withdraw into yourself once more, but retain your connection to the whole through the Amethyst in your hand.
- **Make your way back down the ledge** to where the boatman waits for you. Settle yourself in the boat and allow him to quickly propel the boat back down the narrow river and across the wide shining lake. In front of you, see the point you set out from; soon the boat is tying up at the bank. Thank your boatman for the journey and make your way back onto the bank.
- **When you have finished the journey**, thank the crystal for its light and your guides and helpers for their assistance and ask that they be always with you.
- **Let the light crystallize** at the outer edges of your aura, protecting you within a bubble of light. Take your attention down to your feet. Become very aware of the contact they make with the earth. Feel them holding you and grounding you on the earth and into your body. Then, when you are ready, open your eyes. Don't forget to record your experience in the space provided.

My Amethyst wholeness meditation experience

Date ______________________ **Time** ______________________

My experience ______________________

____

How easily did I surrender to the boatman guiding the journey? ______________________

____

Was the river straight or winding? ______________________

____

Was I content to go with the flow or did I push against the river? ______________________

____

What is my soul path? ______________________

____

How did it feel to be part of the infinity of being? ______________________

____

How did it feel to simply be and go with the flow? ______________________

____

How can I incorporate that beingness into my everyday life? ______________________

____

Was it possible to bring back my connection with the greater whole? ____________

____

How can I maintain the interface between me and the rest of the world? ____________

____

How did it feel to withdraw back into myself? ____________

____

Are there parts of myself that are uncommitted to the journey? ____________

____

Who are my guides and helpers? ____________

____

What do they do for me? ____________

____

Is this still appropriate? ____________

____

Do I need to renegotiate any agreements I made with them? ____________

____

How can they best assist me on my soul path? ____________

____

What other dimensions did I discover to the cave? ____________

____

INSPIRATIONS

You will find these meditations and journeys together with a music-only track in the audio that accompanies this book. Use them as directed in the exercises or let them inspire your own journeys.

AUDIO TRACK 1

Relaxation, focusing and opening the mind's eye

THIS TRACK HELPS YOU TO RELAX, FOCUS AND OPEN YOUR MIND'S EYE

- **Settle yourself in a comfortable place** where you will not be disturbed. Breathe gently and easily, focusing on your breath for 10 breaths. As you breathe out, let go any tension you may be feeling. Pause. And then breathe in a sense of quiet peace.
- **Slowly raise and lower your eyelids** ten times, allowing your eyes to remain closed as you reach the tenth time. Your eyelids feel relaxed and pleasantly heavy. Keeping your eyes closed, raise your eyebrows high and stretch your whole face. Relax and let go. Let the relaxed feeling from your eyelids travel slowly up your forehead and across your scalp, and through all your facial muscles. Smile as widely as you can, move your jaw from side to side, and allow your face to relax.
- **Now lift your shoulders up to your ears** and let go. Allow the relaxed feeling to flow on down through your body. Take a big breath and sigh out any tension you may be feeling. Let your chest and back relax and soften.
- **Clench your fists and let them relax** on your thighs. Allow the sense of relaxation that is passing through your body to go down your arms. Any tension that is left drips out of your fingertips and trickles down to the earth.
- **Pull your belly in, breathing deeply**. Let all your breath out and count to 10. Allow your lower back and abdomen to feel warm and relaxed.
- **Let the feeling of relaxation go** on down through your thighs and knees, flowing down your legs to your feet. Raise and lower your feet and let your calf muscles

be soft and loose. Scrunch your toes up and let them relax. If there is any tension left in your body, allow this to drain out of your feet.

- **You are now feeling comfortably warm** and peaceful, and yet receptive and alert. Spend a few moments enjoying this feeling of total relaxation. Notice how you remain mentally alert but physically relaxed.
- **Now gently focus your attention on your third eye** – the place between and slightly above your eyebrows. Without opening your eyes, look up to this space and sense, feel or see an eye opening there. This is your inner eye, your mind's eye, through which you can use your intuition and focus your intention. This eye opens onto a screen on which you can see images when visualizing. The screen may be behind your third eye or out a foot or so in front of it. Remind yourself that at this moment your intention is to relax while remaining receptive, but that this intention changes, according to the exercise or journey you are undertaking in the future.
- **When you have finished your relaxation**, bring your attention back into your surroundings. Place your feet firmly on the floor and slowly sit up straight. Be aware of your connection with the earth. Get up and move around. If you feel the slightest bit floaty, hold Hematite or place your feet on a brown grounding crystal, such as Smoky Quartz, to connect you to the earth.

AUDIO TRACK 2

Attuning to my crystals

THIS TRACK HELPS YOU TO BRING YOUR ENERGIES INTO UNION WITH THOSE OF A CRYSTAL

- **This track can be used** to get to know any crystal in your collection and to experience its energy. It talks you into a relaxed state, attunes you to the crystal, allows five minutes meditation time to be with the crystal, and then brings you out of the meditation again. Remember that crystal energy is subtle and it may take a little while for you to attune to the vibrations. Learning to recognize how you personally experience crystal energy is an essential first step.
- **Sit quietly holding your cleansed and dedicated crystal**. Breathe gently and allow yourself to relax and focus your attention on the crystal. State your intention to get to know this crystal a little better and to feel its energy.
- **Allow your eyes to go into soft focus** and gaze at the crystal. Note its shape, its colour and size. Follow its contours and craters, if it has a 'window' look inside. Feel how light or heavy the crystal is in your hand. Feel its vibrations and energetic resonance. You may feel your energy jump or tingle – like getting an electric shock – or slow and pulse as it connects to the crystal's energy. Allow the energy of the crystal to travel up your arms and into your heart and mind so that it reveals itself to you.

- **Be aware if the crystal** makes a special contact with any part of your body. If you wish, guide the energy up through your chakras and see if there is an energetic response.
- **If the crystal is transparent or translucent** allow your gaze to pass through the outer edge and into the centre; follow the planes and landscape you find there.
- **When you are ready**, put your crystal down and consciously break off contact with its energies. Open your eyes fully and bring your attention into the room. Take your attention down to your feet and feel the contact they make with the floor. Feel your sit bones make contact with the chair and feel them supporting the weight of your body. Picture a bubble of protection all around you.
- **When you are ready**, stand up and move around, and record your insights.

AUDIO TRACK 4

The Quartz crystal journey

THIS TRACK HELPS YOU TO EXPERIENCE YOUR UNIQUE SENSE OF SELF AND HARNESS WAYS TO EXPRESS YOUR INDIVIDUALITY

- **Sit comfortably and close your eyes.** Without opening your eyes, look up to the point above and between your eyebrows – your 'third eye'. Feel this eye open. Breathe gently and withdraw your attention from the outside world, focusing it deep inside yourself. Hold your Quartz crystal in whichever hand feels comfortable and be aware of its invigorating energy radiating out from the crystal and enfolding you. Feel how it enlivens every cell in your body, energizing and harmonizing as it goes.
- **Let the crystal take you deep down** into the part of you that is independent, individual, separate and personal. Let it show you your ego – the part of you that has desires and drives. This is the place of your will, assertion and aggression. Look carefully at what you are aiming for, what propels you to act as you do. And then look at what holds you back, how and where you procrastinate. Is there anywhere in your life where you always believe you are right no matter what anyone else says? Look, too, at where you are too self-absorbed or selfish to notice other people and their needs.
- **Then let the crystal move you** into the higher part of your being, your own unique Self, the divine part of your being that is housed at the core of your soul. Explore that Self.
- **Let the crystal take you deep down** to its base. Let it show you how it felt when it was part of a larger cluster, when it was part of the whole and connected to everything around it. Move your awareness out so that you too become part of the whole, and then withdraw it back into the birthing of your own unique Self. Find the point of balance between the two.

- **Let the crystal take you deep down** into your Self and connect you to the wisdom of the ages. Ask your Self to examine your shadow qualities with you and to show you what gift lies in the heart of each one and what energy you can reclaim from that shadow that will be useful in your life now.
- **Now feel yourself walking** with that Self, walking your pathway out into the future. As you travel that path, leave gifts for yourself that you will be able to pick up on your life's journey to enable you to express more of your unique Self and fulfil your potential.
- **When you have finished the journey,** bring your attention back into the present moment and picture light crystallizing at the outer edges of your aura, protecting you within a bubble of light.
- **Bring your hand down into your lap** and thank the crystal for its light. Detach from the crystal and put it aside.
- **Take your attention down to your feet.** Be very aware of the contact they make with the earth. Feel them holding you and grounding you on the earth and into your body. Then, when you are ready, open your eyes.

AUDIO TRACK 5

The Rainbow Obsidian journey

THIS TRACK HELPS YOU TO LET GO OF THINGS THAT ARE DETRIMENTAL TO YOUR CURRENT WELL-BEING AND RECOGNIZE YOUR INNER STRENGTHS

- **Settle yourself quietly** and breathe gently, withdrawing your attention from the outside world and into the crystal. Keep your eyes half-open and gaze at the bands of your Rainbow Obsidian. Move the crystal slightly so that it catches the best light to show you the coruscating bands. Feel the strength of the crystal in your hand. Let its energy radiate up your arms and into your heart. As you focus on each band let it take you inwards. Allow the bands to move you gently into contact with your deepest Self. When you feel ready, place the crystal over your heart.
- **Ask the crystal** to let you know what you are holding onto; what it would be beneficial to release. Let it show you any hooks that are in your heart and gently dissolve these, filling the place with fresh energy and forgiveness. Ask the crystal to show you how your past is affecting your present in any area of your life.
- **Then willingly surrender all** that no longer serves you – all the pain and emotions, situations and experiences that have weighed you down and held you back. Acknowledge them and let them be drawn into the crystal for transmutation. Let them go with forgiveness in your heart.
- **Now ask the crystal** to show you the hidden gifts that lay hidden behind that old pain – the qualities you developed and the resources you can draw on. Allow yourself to know how you will use this.

- **Ask the crystal** if it has any other information for you and wait quietly for the answer.
- **Before you begin the return journey** put your attention out to the subtle bodies around your physical body and ask the crystal to draw off and transmute any negative energies or disharmonies, bringing all the subtle bodies into alignment. Then let the crystal draw off and transmute any negative energy, stress or dis-ease in your physical body.
- **Now feel the strong protection** from the crystal that wraps around you in layers.
- **Finally, feel the strength of the crystal** and its powerful connection to the earth grounding and rooting you into your physical existence, bringing you fully into the present moment. When you feel ready, thank the crystal, open your eyes and move around.

Index

A

activating crystals 22
affirmations 220
Agate 30, 83, 84, 98, 99, 127
All That Is 10, 15, 236–40
Amazonite 54
Amber 27, 53, 90, 123
Amethyst 31, 52, 60
  chakras and 83, 84, 90, 98, 99
  geode 218, 236–8
  healing with 147, 155, 156, 159
  massage with 182
  for protection 123
  and spiritual gifts 187
Ammolite 128
amorphous crystals 62, 64
Amphibole 61, 127, 147
Angelite 56
Apache Tear 90
Apophyllite 31, 64, 84
Atlantasite 185
attuning to crystals 44–8, 65, 244–5
  high-vibration 228–31
the aura 15, 90–1, 92, 148
  sensing and cleansing 104–7
Aura Quartzes 210, 211
automatic writing 189
Avalonite geode 60
Aventurine 28, 83, 84, 98, 99, 114, 123, 147
aversion, overcoming 118–19, 138–9
Azeztulite 84, 93, 210, 214

B

ball shapes 58
Banded Agate 151
base chakra 84, 85, 86
bathing with crystals 178, 180–1
bi-coloured crystals 184, 185
Big Crystal Cleanse 42–3
black crystals 57
  Jade 90
  Tourmaline 32, 123, 128, 147
Bloodstone 26, 90, 123
  healing with 147, 152, 155
blue crystals 56
Blue Lace Agate 30, 83, 84, 98, 99, 150
Blue Moonstone 117, 127, 134, 217, 226
body organs 152–7
Brandenberg 93, 108, 109, 214
Bronzite 128
brown crystals 57

C
Cacoxenite 127
Calcite 28
Camelian 27
Carnelian 22, 182
  Orange 83, 84, 98, 99
  Red 114
Cathedral Quartz 10, 147
Celestite 16, 215
chakras 15, 50, 81–112, 114
  and the aura 90–1, 148
  blocked 82
  colours 71, 82, 88–9, 95, 102–3
  exercises 97–112
  and healing 82–3
  opening the higher chakras 92–6, 108–12
  position of 84
  qualities of 86–7
  sensing and cleansing 98–101
Chalcedony Geode 53
channelling (trance) 189
Chlorite Quartz 8
choosing a crystal 17–48
  Crystal Directory 18, 24, 26–32
  exercises 33–48
Chrysocolla 29
Citrine 27, 52, 56, 90, 114
clairaudience/sentience/voyance 189
cleansing chakras 98–101
cleansing crystals 22, 23, 42–3
clear crystals 57
  Quartz 104, 105, 147, 159, 182, 187
cluster shapes 58
colours 52
  chakras 71, 82, 88–9, 95, 102–3
  directory of 54–7
  experiencing 70–3
compassion 114
courage 114
crown chakra 84, 85, 87
Crystal Directory 18, 24, 26–32
  high-vibration 214–17
crystal energies 50, 53
  feeling 65, 66–9
crystal qualities 114–15, 116
crystal systems 62–4
  exploring 78–80
Crystalline Hemimorphite 54
cubic crystals 62, 63

D
Dalmation Stone 185
Danburite 63, 84, 93, 108, 109, 147, 214, 220
  attracting love 222, 232, 233
detoxification layout 155, 170–3
Dioptase 84, 93, 108
dis-ease 15, 16
  and chakras 82, 83
  sources of 146–7
double-terminated crystals 58
dowsing 21, 40–1, 124, 204

E

earth chakra 84, 85, 86
earth star chakra 94, 95
egg-shaped crystals 59, 182
elestial shapes 59
Emerald 63
emotional healing 148–9
etheric blueprint 15
exploring crystal systems 78–80
eye crystals 8–10

F

figure-of-eight grid 127
finger dowsing 21, 40–1, 204
five-pointed star 126
Flint 18, 90
Fluorite 31, 54, 57, 90
  for healing 147
  for protection 121, 122, 140

G

Gamet 26
Gaspeite 121
gem essences 180, 190–2, 204–8
generator shapes 59
geodes 60, 218, 236
geopathic stress 15
Graspeite 185
green crystals 56, 121, 140
  Aventurine 83, 84, 98, 99, 114, 123, 140, 147
  Tourmaline 32, 147
Greenlandite 117, 134
grey crystals 57
grid systems 15, 124–8, 142–4
Grossular Garnet 128
groups of crystals 62–4

H

Halite 26, 180
healing 15, 145–76
  body organs 152–7, 170–3
  and chakras 82–3
  Crystal Directory of 26–32
  emotional 148–9
  exercises 161–76
  with gem essences 204–8
  immune system 146–7, 162–5
  the mind 158–60, 174–6
  releasing from the past 150–1, 166–9
heart chakra 84, 85, 87
heart seed chakra 84, 85, 94, 95
Hematite 32, 138
hexagonal crystals 62, 63
high-vibration crystals 16, 24, 93
  figure-of-eight grid 127
  working with 210–17, 226–31
higher crown chakra 94, 95
higher heart chakra 84, 85, 94, 95
higher vibration chakras 92, 94–6
  activation exercise 108–12

I

Identifying my Crystals 34–9
immune system 146–7, 162–5
indigo crystals 57
inner wisdom 188
intuition v0, 188
intuitive crystal selection 20–1, 40–1
Iron Pyrite 157

J K

Jade 29, 90, 114, 117, 121, 140
Jasper 27, 156, 185
  Red 83, 84, 88, 98, 104, 114, 155, 182
  Yellow 83, 84, 98, 99, 155
Jet 90
journal-keeping 12–14
journeys 16, 218, 246–9
Kunzite 90, 114
Kyanite 30

L

Labradonite 64, 90, 104, 159, 187, 215, 226
  for protection 120, 122
Lapis Lazuli 30, 54, 157
Lemurian 117, 134, 214
lightbody 16, 92, 210
lilac crystals 57
love, attracting 220, 222–4, 232–5
love baths 180

M

Malachite 28, 56, 150
massage 180, 182–3, 196–7
meditation 178, 194–5, 236–40
Merlinite 117, 134, 185
the mind 158–60, 174–6
Mohave Turquoise 52
Moldavite 51, 214
monoclinic crystals 62, 63
Moss Agate 28
Mystic Topaz 117, 134

N O

Natural Pumice 54
Natural Spirit Quartz 54
Nirvana Quartz 93, 108, 109, 217
Obsidian 53, 64, 150, 151
orange crystals 55
  Carnelian 83, 84, 98, 99
orthorhombic crystals 62, 63

P

Paraiba Tourmaline 210, 211, 214
past life chakra 87
Pelatite 84
Peridot 29
Petalite 93, 108, 109, 216
phantoms 60
Phenacite 93, 108, 109, 214
physical anatomy 152, 153
pink crystals 55
points 60

Polished Malachite 54
Poppy Jasper 127
portals 8
Prasiolite 52
precognition 188
Preseli Bluestone 53, 84, 93, 108, 109
protection crystals 120–8
psychic immune system 146–7
psychokinesis 188
psychometry 189
purple crystals 57
Pyrolusite 90
Quantum Quattro 140
Quartz 22, 31, 210, 226
  Crystal Journey 115, 130–3, 246–7
  shapes 58, 59, 60, 61

R

Rainbow Moonstone 210
Rainbow Obsidian 150, 151, 166–9
  journey 248–9
rational crystal selection 20
raw crystals 18, 54
recording your experiences 12–14
red crystals 53, 55, 114
Red Jasper 114, 182
  chakras and 83, 84, 88, 98, 104
  healing with 155
relaxation 10, 242–3
remote viewing 189
retrocognition v188
Rhodochrosite 118, 150, 182
rituals 218–24
Rose Quartz 26, 84, 114
  attracting love 220, 222, 232
  dispelling fear 118, 138
  healing 147
  love baths 180
  massage with 182
  for protection 120, 123

S

sacral chakra 84, 85, 86
Satyamani 108, 217
Sayaloka Quartz 108
sceptres 61
Selenite 8, 63, 90, 104, 123, 216
self-development 113–44
  crystal qualities 114–15, 130–3
  crystals I avoid 118–19, 138–9
  crystals I love 116–17, 134–7
  exercises 129–44
self-protection 120–3, 140–1
Septarian 30, 83, 84, 98, 99, 127
shapes of crystals 52–3
  directory of 58–61
Shiva Lingham 185, 198–9
Smithsonite 147
Smoky Quartz 32, 52
  aura 104
  chakras 83, 84, 90, 93, 98, 108
  healing with 155, 159
  overcoming aversion to 118, 138–9

for protection 118, 122
Snakeskin Agate 152, 157
Snow Quartz 18, 57
Sodalite 83, 98, 99, 123, 187
healing with 147, 155, 159
solar plexus chakra 84, 85, 86
solar star chakra 84, 85
soma chakra 84, 85, 94, 95
soul star chakra 94, 96, 210
space, protecting 124–8, 142–4
Spirit Quartz 214
spiritual gifts 186–9, 202–3
spleen chakra 84, 85, 86
spleen protection 121, 140–1
square crystals 60
Star of David 126, 128
stellar gateway chakra 84, 85, 94, 96, 210
Stibnite 8
storing crystals 23
Sugilite 30

T

talking to crystals 184–5, 198–201
Tanzanite 210, 215
telepathy 188
tetragonal crystals 62, 64
third eye chakra 84, 85, 87
throat chakra 84, 85, 87
Tiger's Eye 57, 114
Topaz 117, 134
Tourmaline 32, 64, 90, 123, 128, 147
toxic crystal esssences 190
triangulation 126
triclinic crystals 62, 64
trigonal crystals 62, 64
Tugtupeite 93, 108, 109, 210, 211, 216
tumbled crystals 18, 54, 61, 182
Turquoise 29, 122
twin crystals 61

V W

Variscite 84
visualization 10
Vivianite 8–10
wands 8, 53, 61, 182
white crystals 57
working with crystals 178–208
exercises 193–208

Y Z

yellow crystals 56
Jasper 83, 84, 98, 99, 155
zig-zag layout 126
Zincite 51
Zoisite egg 59

Acknowledgements

I would like to thank all the participants on my workshops who have helped to shape how I work with crystals. I have learned much from you all, and from all the crystal suppliers who introduce me to new crystals as they arrive. Finally, as always, thanks to David Eastoe (www.petaltone.co.uk) without whose cleansing essences I could not work.

Executive Editor: Sandra Rigby

Editor: Ruth Wiseall

Deputy Creative Director: Karen Sawyer

Designer: Cobalt

Assistant Production Controller: Vera Janke

Picture Research: Marian Sumega

Picture credits: Alamy Image Source Black 1. **Fotolia** aarnet 89. **Octopus Publishing Group** 2, 4, 6, 9, 10, 16, 17, 19, 23, 26, 27, 28, 29, 30, 31, 32, 49, 51, 53, 55, 56, 57, 58, 59, 60, 61, 63, 64, 81, 93, 113, 115, 117, 119, 122, 123, 124, 145, 150, 155, 156, 157, 159, 177, 179, 180, 182, 183, 185, 186, 209, 211, 212, 213, 216, 217, 218, 220, 223; /Andy Komorowski 21; /Frazer Cunningham 146; /Mike Prior 25, 83, 120, 125, 148; /Russell Sadur 13, 14, 91, 181, 191, 192, 219, 221

THEMES OF THE PLAY

1. '*Nature*'

King Lear is the story of the disasters which happened when an old man gave his kingdom to his daughters, and shows how completely he misunderstood them, and how he tried to keep his power though he had abandoned his responsibilities. Shakespeare uses the story as an opportunity to discuss many themes, among them the whole question of relationships between parents and children, and between rulers and ruled, and to explore the various meanings which people give to the words 'nature' and 'natural'.

The Elizabethan audience were not only looking at a stage very different from ours, they were looking at it from a different moral standpoint. We may well be troubled by the state of the world today, muddled, chaotic, unjust, at sixes and sevens: but we expect it to be like that. The Elizabethans too noted the disorders in their world: civil war on the Continent, religious strife and conspiracy at home and abroad, threat of invasion, rising prices, exorbitant rents, crowds of beggars—but they regarded all these things as extraordinary, wrong and (as the Duke of Burgundy says when describing war-shattered France) 'everything that seems unnatural'. (*Henry V*, V 2 62).

Most Elizabethans believed that the universe, the globe, the country they lived in should all, 'naturally' be orderly and harmonious. God had planned a universe, the earth at the centre with the stars and planets swinging harmoniously round it, each in its place. On earth similarly the king, the nobility and the ordinary people should move in their appointed ways, never straying. Everyone and everything from God himself to the meanest living creature, and even to plants and stones, had an allotted place in this 'great chain of being', as it was called, 'which order', wrote Edmund Dudley, 'God willeth us firmly to keep'.

This is an Elizabethan commonplace, repeated in the officially-prescribed Homilies which were used as sermons, in political and ecclesiastical writings, and in poems and plays. Machiavelli had challenged this view of politics, and Copernicus had doubted its picture of the heavens, but it was still very widely accepted. If any single part of the universe moved out of place, then everything else would be affected too. The movement of the fixed stars circling regularly round the pole corresponded with the course of nature, the regular circle of the seasons, growth and decay. The planets, which (until Galileo observed them through a telescope in 1610) were thought to be stars moving erratically, matched the visibly more erratic lives of men and nations. Really unusual appearances in the heavens—comets or eclipses—were warnings of tragedies on earth. After Othello has murdered his wife, he cries:

> Methinks it should be now a huge eclipse
> Of sun and moon. (*Othello* V 2 98)

Old Gloucester in *Lear* is distraught by the extraordinary goings-on in the kingdom:

> Kent banished thus? and France in choler parted?
> And the king gone tonight? Prescribed his power?
> (I 2 23)

Then his wicked bastard son Edmund tricks Gloucester into thinking that his good son Edgar is rebelling against him. Gloucester exclaims:

> These late eclipses in the sun and moon portend no good to us. . . . Love cools, friendship falls off, brothers divide. In cities, mutinies; in countries, discord; in palaces, treason; and the bond cracked 'twixt son and father. This villain of mine comes under the prediction; there's son against father: the king falls from the bias of nature; there's father against child. (I 2 106).

In this speech Gloucester sums up the 'ruinous disorders' (I 2 116) which are the theme of the play. Lear's love for Cordelia cools; friendship falls off between Lear and Kent, eventually between Goneril and Regan; the brothers Edmund and Edgar divide. There is mutiny and discord when the French army lands in England; Lear and Gloucester both find treason in palaces; both find the bond cracked between father and child.

Later we see Edmund telling his brother that 'those eclipses do portend these divisions' (I 2 139). And he too foresees disasters*:

> *Unnaturalness* between the child and the parent, death, dearth, dissolutions of ancient amities, divisions in state, menaces and maledictions against kings and nobles, . . . banishments of friends . . . nuptial breaches. (I 2 147).

But though he accurately foretells the course of events to come, this is not what Edmund really believes. When alone, soliloquising and giving us his own genuine views, he mocks his father's belief in astrology. Edmund thinks that we bring our troubles on ourselves, but, unwilling to be responsible, prefer to blame the innocent stars.

* disasters: aster means star: dis-aster means literally an unfavourable aspect of a star or planet, hence the modern meaning of the word derives from the idea that unfavourable stars led to very unpleasant happenings.

> When we are sick in fortune, often the surfeits of our own behaviour, we make guilty of our disasters the sun, the moon and stars; as if we were villains on necessity, fools by heavenly compulsion, knaves, thieves and treachers by spherical predominance, drunkards, liars and adulterers by an enforced obedience of planetary influence, and all that we are evil in by a divine thrusting on. . . . My father compounded with my mother under the Dragon's tail, and my nativity was under Ursa Major, so that it follows I am rough and lecherous. But, I should have been that I am, had the maidenliest star in the firmament twinkled on my bastardizing. (I 2 122).

We may note that in Shakespeare's plays it is only the rebels like Edmund, Cassius (*Julius Caesar* I 2 139–40) and Hotspur (*I Henry IV*, III 1 13 ff.), men who are trying to upset authority on earth, who refuse to acknowledge the power of the stars, which symbolises the rule of order in the universe.

The 'bias of nature' (I 2 14), that is, *natural* behaviour, means to Gloucester love and loyalty between parents and children. A son should be a 'loyal and natural boy' (II 1 84); when Gloucester is blinded he expects that 'nature' will make his son revenge him (III 7 85), though we may wonder if his slighting references to Edmund (I 1 8–23) are likely to have awakened a son's love and loyalty. But when Edmund pretends that Edgar has the 'unnatural purpose' to kill their father, and declares

> with how manifold and strong a bond
> The child was bound to the father, (II 1 47)

we know that Edmund is ironically pretending, to deceive his father, that he holds the orthodox view: we have already heard him, when alone, giving his true opinion.

Thou, Nature, art my Goddess, (I 2 1)

cries Edmund, but to *him* 'natural man' is selfish, self-seeking man, man without checks or restraints, out for all he can get regardless of anyone else's interests.

Edmund here may be thought to represent the 'New Men' in Tudor England. The old feudal nobility stepped 'naturally', by birth, into positions of importance; but these new men were making their way upward, often unscrupulously, by sheer ability. In a play by Dekker the 'city doctrine' is defined:

Nature sent man into the world, alone,
Without all company, but to care for one—

and that one, himself. This doctrine is exemplified both in the words and in the behaviour of Shakespeare's Richard III. Inevitably such men rejected a static society in which no one moved from his proper, original, station. To them, the 'natural' world was a jungle; their 'nature' was red in tooth and claw, and might was right. This is the world in which Falstaff justifies himself for defrauding Mr. Justice Shallow by appealing to 'nature':

If the young dace be a bait for the old pike, I see no reason in the law of nature but I may snap at him.
(2 *Henry IV*, III 2 357)

This is the world of Edmund, Goneril and Regan. As soon as Lear has no power, they cease to respect him.

I pray you, father, being weak, seem so, (II 4 197)

says Regan, and she would rather please her powerful sister Goneril than her powerless dethroned father (II 2 142–7).

But to the more orthodox Elizabethan a father, even in extreme weakness, was worthy of a daughter's respect, and should receive it. Theseus instructs Hermia, in *A Midsummer Night's Dream*,

To you your father should be as a god. (I 1 47)

The horror of Lear's story was the *unnatural* behaviour of Goneril and Regan. They are daughters who revolt against their father, subjects who revolt against their king, sisters who betray each other, wives who betray their husbands; these are not only personal sins, but an upsetting of the divine order of the universe, as reflected in the rightly ordered family and the rightly governed state. The natural order, as Lear says, implies

The offices of nature, bond of childhood,
Effects of courtesy, dues of gratitude. (II 4 174)

When Regan puts her father's messenger in the stocks, Lear thinks

'tis worse than murder
To do upon respect such violent outrage. (II 4 22)

A daughter who disregards or disowns her father can never flourish. Albany realises with horror his wife's true disposition:

That nature which contemns its origin
Cannot be bordered certain in itself.
She that herself will sliver and disbranch
From her material sap, perforce must wither
And come to deadly use. (IV 2 32)

The 'unkindness' of Lear's daughters and Gloucester's son is more than cruelty; they are, as well as being cruel, not behaving like kindred, not like their species, mankind.

I tax not you, you elements, with *unkindness*, (III 2 16)

cries Lear, battered by wind and rain; for the elements are only behaving as elements should, doing their kind:

Nor rain, wind, thunder, fire are my daughters. (III 2 15)

Daughters should 'naturally' be dutiful, affectionate—

> Is there any cause in nature that makes these hard hearts? (III 6 75).

An 'unkind daughter' (III 4 70) is 'degenerate' (I 4 254 and IV 2 44), less than human (IV 2 40), in fact a monster (III 7 101). Again we are told that ingratitude 'in a child' is 'more hideous than the sea-monster' (I 4 260–2); and we must remember that the word 'monster' to an Elizabethan meant something deformed, something utterly inhuman, a personification of some monstrous vice. (See IV 2 59–61, 62–3 and I 5 39).

To most Elizabethans, it seemed that 'children' should be 'kind and natural' (*Henry V*, Prol. to Act II, 19), and in this sort of world, the world of Cordelia, Edgar, Gloucester, Kent and (eventually) of Lear, the 'natural' attributes are love, charity, order, concord, harmony. The conflict between the two opposed views of what is 'natural', of what 'Nature' means, is basic in the play. The characters are divided as clearly as in a Western—perhaps the modern equivalent of the morality play—into 'good' people and 'bad' people, holding opposite beliefs; and in the end, though only a few of the good live happily ever after, all the bad perish.

Further Reading:

E. M. W. Tillyard, *The Elizabethan World Picture* (A most readable and clear exposition of the orthodox idea of 'the great chain of being'.)

J. F. Danby, *Shakespeare's Doctrine of Nature* (Different views of Nature, discussed with special reference to *King Lear*).

George Herbert, *Man*. This poem is a Christian expression of the view of nature as an ordered world, and of man's responsibility for playing his part in it.

Questions:

1. Remembering that the actual speeches in the play are not spoken by Shakespeare, but by his characters, can we discover which view of the natural world (as orderly and harmonious, or as a fierce jungle) was held by Shakespeare himself?

2. Disorder is unnatural and wrong. How does Shakespeare illustrate this in *King Lear*? What different types of disorder are shown?

2. '*Patience*'.

We can trace other traditional ideas and influences in *King Lear*. If we consider the play not only as a study of man as a member of society, or of a family, but as a study of man as an individual, we see that in some ways the pattern of the play resembles that of the old morality play, *Everyman*. Everyman is deserted by those who owe him most, Kindred and Fellowship; his Worldly Goods go from him; he is rescued and regenerated (after he has repented and been punished) by the representatives of goodness. It is quite clear that he must patiently endure punishment before he can be saved.

The idea that patient endurance was the highest human virtue came from the ancient Stoic philosophers, and at the end of the sixteenth century such Stoics as Marcus Aurelius and Seneca were much discussed and admired. They believed that man should live according to Nature, and that the most striking thing about nature was its order: a man's duty, then, was to find out what his natural place should be, and then fill it to the best of his ability. He must be master of himself, and his reason must rule his passions; he must accept calmly and patiently whatever life had in store for him. And we may think that *King Lear* is a play about man's endurance of suffering, and about the patience he sometimes acquires while enduring. In fact, how he becomes a stoic. It can also be seen as a play about the regeneration of the human heart.

Cordelia and Edgar, the good children, seem to be naturally patient; to possess themselves in patience, to wait patiently upon the will of the gods, trusting that in due time things will improve, or at least work out to some intelligible ending. 'Men must endure,' says Edgar (V 2 10). Gloucester cries in despair:

> As flies to wanton boys are we to th' gods;
> They kill us for their sport. (IV 1 36)

But to Edgar it seems that

> The gods are just, and of our pleasant vices
> Make instruments to plague us: (V 3 169)

our suffering is the result of our earlier mistakes: if Gloucester had not sinned in begetting Edmund, he would not have been betrayed and blinded.

Both fathers, Lear and Gloucester, are impulsive, and act before thinking. 'Pray, sir, be patient' (I 4 262) says Albany when Lear is maddened by Goneril's disrespect, and 'I pray you sir, take patience' (II 4 134) says Regan in her turn. And though Lear says that he 'can be patient' (II 4 226), demands 'patience—patience' (II 4 267) from the heavens and declares that he 'will be the pattern of all patience' (III 2 37), this is a wildly incongruous boast in the midst of his impatient ravings. 'Sir,' asks Kent,

> Sir, where is the patience now
> That you so oft have boasted to retain? (III 6 57)

The Fool says in one of his songs that man

Must make content with his fortunes fit; (III 2 76)

Lear agrees, 'True, boy'; but the play shows Lear in a continual state of rebellion against the fortune which he has, to a very considerable extent, made for himself.

Lear suffers apparently to the limit of endurance. He will not bend, so he is broken. But how much can man endure? How can misery be measured? Edgar asks the gods

Who is't can say 'I am at the worst'? (IV 1 25)

and answers that

... the worst is not
So long as we can say, 'This is the worst'; (IV 1 27)

for torment can be continued until man is speechless. Gloucester envies Lear his madness, as making him less conscious of his woes. Through torment Gloucester learned to bear

Affliction till it do cry out itself
'Enough, enough,' and die; (IV 6 75)

and to bear, in another sense, 'free and *patient* thoughts' (IV 6 80). After his attempt to kill himself has failed, Gloucester resigns himself to his fate—

You ever gentle gods, take my breath from me;
Let not my worser spirit tempt me again
To die before you please! (IV 6 215)

And Lear also, though very slowly, does learn to endure—'Pour on, I will endure' (III 4 18), he says, enduring not only the external tempest, but the suffering inflicted on his pride, his whole ego. Lear suffers till he can endure no more, and goes mad. Then with what Edgar calls 'reason in madness' Lear preaches to Gloucester:

Thou must be patient. We came crying hither;

Thou know'st the first time that we smell the air
We wawl and cry. (IV 6 177)

Both Lear and Gloucester learn through suffering; being outcast, they learn to pity 'poor naked wretches' (III 4 28). Gloucester realises that it is not enough for 'the *superfluous* and lust-dieted man' (IV 1 66) merely to see, without actually experiencing, poverty—he

will not see
Because he does not *feel*. (IV 1 67)

Only experience will teach him that he should share his extra wealth—

So distribution should undo excess,
And each man have enough. (IV 6 69)

Notice how closely Gloucester echoes, both in thought and language, Lear's earlier command to himself:

Take physic, pomp;
Expose thyself to *feel* what wretches *feel*,
That thou mayst shake the *superflux* to them
And show the heavens more just. (III 4 33)

Edgar, describing his own experience, describes at the same time that of his father and of the king:

A most poor man, made tame to Fortune's blows,
Who by the art of known and *feeling* sorrows
Am pregnant to good pity. (IV 6 219)

It is only through the actual experience of suffering that Lear and Gloucester learn to feel sympathy.

In concentration camps, when those being tortured faint, they are revived only in order to undergo more torture. And this is what happened to Lear. He is revived, restored, reconciled with Cordelia; only to be captured once more, imprisoned—which seems to him unimportant, if he is to be with Cordelia—and finally to suffer the ultimate blow, her death. And when he dies,

The wonder is he hath endured so long. (V 3 316)

'The oldest hath borne most' (V 3 325), says Edgar;

we that are young
Shall never see so much, nor live so long.

Further Reading:

Edwin Muir, *The Politics of 'King Lear'*, in *Essays on Literature and Society* (1949).

George Orwell, *Lear, Tolstoy and the Fool*, in his *Selected Essays* (Penguin).

Questions:

1. Trace the stages of Lear's suffering, and the corresponding changes in his character.

2. 'Prosperity doth best discover vice, but Adversity doth best discover virtue'. (Bacon) How is this illustrated by *King Lear*? Give examples of incidents from the play which justify Bacon's remark.

3. 'Crabbed age and youth cannot live together.' Show how Shakespeare illustrates the differences in outlook between the old and the young.

4. Coleridge said that '*Lear* is the only serious performance of Shakespeare the interest and situations of which are derived from the assumption of a gross improbability'. A German critic, Rümelin, wrote in 1866 about the action in *King Lear*: 'Nursery stories are not fit subjects for tragedy'. Does the 'gross improbability' of the bare plot, or the fact of its being a 'nursery story' (Once upon a time there lived a king who had three daughters . . .) seem to you unfortunate? Is there any reason why such plots should not be used when a playwright wishes to discuss serious questions?

THE PLAY ON THE STAGE

1. *Changes in the Physical Theatre*

Shakespeare was the most successful playwright—and 'wright' means craftsman—of his day, attached to the leading company of actors. And *King Lear* is often described as this great playwright's greatest play. So it is surprising to find many critics agreeing with Charles Lamb that 'The *Lear* of Shakespeare cannot be acted,' or with the great critic Bradley that *King Lear* is 'too huge for the stage'.

This would certainly have surprised Shakespeare, since in his day plays were not written to be read but to be acted; half of his plays were not published until seven years after his death. A play was written for a particular company. If it was printed, any rival company could act it, so it was only in financial emergencies that companies sold their plays to a printer. When Ben Jonson published his *Works* in 1616, the year of Shakespeare's death, people were amused because he dared to include his plays as *reading* matter.

But let us remember that Shakespeare wrote *King Lear* for a particular kind of stage at a particular time: theatrical conditions had completely changed in the two hundred years between Shakespeare and Lamb, and changed again in the hundred years between Lamb and Bradley. We must note also that from 1681 till the early nineteenth century the play that was acted as *King Lear* was not Shakespeare's, but a version largely rewritten by Nahum Tate (1652–1715); and even at the end of the nineteenth century, Bradley could only see a much shortened and rearranged version of the play on the professional stage.

Scholars differ about the details of the Elizabethan public theatre, but the general features are agreed. A large fore-stage had the audience closely grouped round it; the actors could appear also in a curtained recess or inner stage, at the back of the great stage, or on a balcony or balconies above it.

There was no way of shutting off the great stage from the audience, so at the end of a tragedy the curtain could not be dropped to hide the bodies—there had to be a funeral procession and some short speeches to cover their removal. Opportunity was usually taken to assure the audience that though great men might die, the world would still go on—Macbeth was slain, but a new king would be crowned at Scone; Hamlet was dead, but Fortinbras would govern Denmark; and despite the deaths of Lear and Cordelia, Edgar would

> Rule in this realm and the gored state sustain.
>
> (V 3 30)

There was no changeable pictorial scenery: the same permanent structure always backed the stage: two big doors, and between them tapestry curtains covering the recess beneath the balcony. All the woodwork, probably, was richly carved and painted. The audience saw something rather like the end of a college hall or one of the halls of the Inns of Court. Two great pillars (in one theatre, the *Swan*, marbled and with imposing capitals) held up the 'shadow' or 'heavens', a structure which sheltered part of the stage—for otherwise the theatre was open to the sky.

The illusion of place was created by the characters themselves and by their words and actions. If the important thing about a scene was simply the encounter of characters, often there would be no indication of place. It did not matter where, particularly, they met. If the place mattered, the dramatist would indicate it, or sometimes describe it, to the audience. Duncan and Banquo describe Macbeth's castle (*Macbeth* I 6 1–10). Quince says in *Midsummer Night's Dream*, '. . . here's a marvellous convenient place for our rehearsal. This green plot shall be our stage, this hawthorn brake our tiring-house . . .' (III 1 2)—tiring-house means dressing-room. In *Henry V* the Chorus is used to set the various scenes. When a king appears in state we can deduce, even if there is not a throne in the inner recess behind him, that he is in his palace, as in the opening scene of *King Lear*.

In *King Lear* neither century nor place is ever clearly stated and this, on Shakespeare's kind of stage, helps to give the play a universal, rather than a period or localised, atmosphere. Productions have been placed in many centuries from the eighth onwards, and in many countries; recently producers have set the play in classical Japan (1956) and among Eskimos (1961). But such notions are apt to distract the audience by their ingenuity, and to detract from the timeless quality of the play.

The eighteenth and nineteenth century stage was very different from Shakespeare's. It was a box, cut off from the audience by a proscenium arch, and still more perhaps by the footlights and the row of audience-repelling spikes round the edge of the stage. Illusion was attempted by means of painted shutter scenery, or pictorial backcloths and wings, which grew more and more elaborate as the nineteenth century drew on; and often when the scene was changed there was a pause while heavy scenery was shifted and rearranged.

How did this change affect *King Lear*? First, this greatly lengthened the performance. To have time for changes of scenery, much of the text had to be cut. Then actor-managers (there were no 'producers' in the modern sense until the twentieth century) attempted to save time by altering the order of scenes. It became the practice on the picture stage, where a realistic 'heath' has to be twice replaced by 'a room in Gloucester's castle', to run the storm scenes together, to save scene-changing—as if Shakespeare did not know his business at all—and to put the scenes in the castle together elsewhere, or else to omit them*. Shakespeare breaks up the storm scenes, deliberately, both to give the actor playing Lear some breathing space—which Sir John Gielgud has told us is essential in the part—and also to contrast storm and calm, to parallel the betrayal of Gloucester with the downfall of Lear, the physical violence and horror of Gloucester's blinding with the spiritual blows which have broken Lear. On the unlocalised stage of Shakespeare's theatre, the change of scene presented no difficulty at all.

In *King Lear* there are four central scenes, three in open country (III 1, 2, 4), usually described as a 'heath' since Shakespeare's editor Rowe so called it in 1708, and one in a hovel near by (III 6). Between and after them come three scenes in a castle (III 3, 5, 7). On a stage without pictorial scenery, Kent and a Gentleman manage to establish in a few lines that they are searching for the king, and in a storm.

Who's there besides foul weather?

* Macready in 1838 put III 6 in the middle of III 4. Irving too ran these scenes together. Bradley said that 'in our present theatres . . . the three storm scenes are usually combined, with disastrous effect'. And again: 'the "cuts" necessitated by modern scenery would have made [the subplot] absolutely unintelligible to me if I had not been familiar with it.'

> . . . Where's the King?
> Contending with the fretful elements . . .
> . . . the to-and-fro conflicting wind and rain.
> This night, wherein the cub-drawn bear would couch . . . (III 1 1 ff.)

When they go off, Lear can enter at once, creating the full fury of the storm with his words:

> Blow, winds, and crack your cheeks! rage! blow!
> You cataracts and hurricanoes, spout
> Till you have drenched our steeples, drowned the cocks!
> You sulph'rous and thought-executing fires,
> Vaunt-couriers of oak-cleaving thunderbolts,
> Singe my white head! (III 2 1)

And the Fool's cringing from the wet adds to the illusion:

> O nuncle, court holy-water in a dry house is better than this rainwater out o' door. Good nuncle, in; ask thy daughters blessing! Here's a night pities neither wise men nor fools. (III 2 10)

At the end of the scene Kent leads Lear off to shelter, and Gloucester and Edmund can at once appear in 'mine own house' (as Gloucester says), perhaps appearing in the inner recess as its curtains are drawn back. As soon as the conversation ends, Lear returns with Kent and the Fool, and we are with them once more on the heath where, Kent informs us,

> The tyranny of the open night's too rough
> For nature to endure. (III 4 2)

Thus the howling storm alternates with the snugness of the castle, to which we return to see Gloucester's downfall, plotted by his false son. Then we are again with Lear, imagining himself judging his false daughters. We leave him blind and senseless and yet again go back to the castle where Gloucester too—this time literally—loses his eyes. The crescendo of Lear's suffering, set against the parallel story of Gloucester, is all one. Tension is maintained; there are no slack pauses while stage hands shift scenery and the audience relax and chat.

And indeed the storm in Lear himself and in Shakespeare's poetry is far greater than any 'wind-machine' or 'thunder-sheet' could contrive. Lear *is* the storm. His passions, like Cleopatra's, are 'greater storms and tempests than almanacs can report' (*Antony and Cleopatra* I 2 159). Lear himself says,

> this tempest in my mind
> Doth from my senses take all feeling else
> Save what beats there. (III 4 12)

The outer storm is, comparatively, unimportant. And the more realistic the stage effects—as in the famous 'land-storm' which drowned Kean's voice in the Drury Lane production of 1820—the less we are seeing and hearing the Lear of Shakespeare.

Further Reading:

E. K. Chambers, *The Elizabethan Stage* (4 vols) and G. E. Bentley, *The Jacobean and Caroline Stage* (5 vols) (Invaluable as works of reference for selective reading).

J. C. Adams, *The Globe Playhouse* (2nd edn. 1961) and C. W. Hodges, *The Globe Restored* (attempted reconstructions of Shakespeare's own theatre).

Questions:

1. Choose several successive scenes in *King Lear* and consider how you would have produced them on the Elizabethan stage. Read the beginning of each scene carefully to see whether Shakespeare identifies its setting, and if so, how he does this. Compare your ideas with

Adams, *The Globe Playhouse*, pp. 385–403, an attempted description of the 1605–6 production. Is it really likely that the important scene of Gloucester's blinding would be played on the balcony? Suggest an alternative scheme.

2. Consider the incongruities in *King Lear*—an early British society with Dukes and Earls, with Elizabethan customs, with pagan oaths and Christian references. Find examples of these, and other, incongruities. Are producers justified in setting the play in one particular country or century? How would you set and dress *King Lear* today?

2. *Reading and Seeing the Play*

How much of the play is lost to the mere reader? The audience actually sees Edgar as a naked beggar (II 3), and this must add point and poignancy to the references to nakedness and beggars in Lear's speech in the immediately following scene (II 4 260 ff.). Again, it is a very gifted reader who can silently hear, as he reads of Lear's restoration to sanity, the accompanying music (IV 7 25 ff.). No reading of stage directions can shock the reader as the audience (the *hearers*) are shocked by the actual sound of Edmund's questioning trumpet and Edgar's answering blast (V 3 110 ff.) which has been compared by Mr. G. Wilson Knight to the last trump.

Shakespeare's words often demand corresponding action to complete them: for instance, Lear's attempt to discover if he sleeps or wakes:

> I will not swear these are my hands: let's see: I feel this pin prick; (IV 7 55)

or his weakness—'Pray you, undo this button' (V 3 309).

Shakespeare's use of words is unsurpassed, yet words are not everything. Perhaps Cordelia's most moving appearance is her last, silent and dead in her father's arms. And though Shakespeare is content to describe the death of Gloucester, Lear's death is shown.

Questions:

1. Read IV 6 85 ff. (Nature's above art . . . Pass.') How much, if anything, does the *reader* of this passage lose? Note that Edgar describes Lear, here, as 'thou side-piercing *sight*' (IV 6 85). Find other passages where action is clearly indicated.

2. Read IV 6 215 ('You ever gentle gods') to 228 ('destroy thee'). What is Gloucester's physical attitude, here? Would a reader be likely to miss this?

3. *Shakespeare's Dramatic Skill*

As one example of Shakespeare's skill as a dramatist we might consider how he used an idea from a scene in the old play *King Leir*, which was one of his sources. Leir and Perillus (Kent's forerunner) escape to Brittany, and tell their sad tale to the disguised Cordella and her husband, the Gallian king. Leir says that he has come to sue to his dismissed daughter, and Cordella reassures him:

Cordella:

Myself a father have a great way hence,
Used me as ill as ever you did her;
Yet, that his reverend age I once might see,
I'd creep along, to meet him on my knee.

Leir:

O, no men's children are unkind but mine.

Cordella:

Condemn not all, because of others' crime:
But look, dear father, look, behold and see
Thy loving daughter speaketh unto thee.

(She kneels)

Leir:

O stand thou up, it is my part to kneel. . . .

Leir kneels in turn, Cordella bids him rise, which he does, but kneels again, rises again, and down goes Cordella—

But I will never rise from off my knee
Until I have your blessing. . . .

And then the Gallian king and his courtier also kneel and rise, the whole series of gestures being extended almost ludicrously. What does Shakespeare make of all this?

Shakespeare's Lear, recovering his senses, uncertain if he is asleep or awake, alive or dead, finds himself royally robed, in a chair of state. Cordelia kneels at his feet, reminding us perhaps that last time they were together she was banished without a blessing (I 1 263–4). When Lear attempts to rise and kneel with, or to, her, she cries with great tenderness,

No, sir, you must not kneel, (IV 7 59)

thus reminding us of Lear's mock kneeling to Regan, and her scorn of his 'unsightly tricks' (II 4 150 ff.) In the last act we hear Lear's final solution and resolution of the situation:

When thou dost ask me blessing, I'll kneel down
And ask of thee forgiveness. (V 3 10)

It is the memory of these earlier words and gestures which completes the total effect of Lear's words—words echoed by Blake—

And throughout all eternity
I forgive you, you forgive me.

As another example of sheer dramatic skill, this time in the creation of suspense, we might consider the last scene of the play, remembering that anyone in the Jacobean audience who knew the story from the Chronicles, or from the old play *King Leir*, would expect Cordelia to mount the throne, as she does in those earlier versions of the tale.

We hear at the end of V 2 that

King Lear hath lost: he and his daughter ta'en.

We see Lear and Cordelia sent to prison while Edmund (who has earlier declared that he will never pardon them (V 1 65 ff.)) gives secret sinister orders, to be carried out 'instantly', to a favourite captain. Albany demands Lear and Cordelia, but is put off. While Edmund is fought over by Goneril and Regan, Regan poisoned, Goneril's wickedness exposed, and Edmund challenged and fatally wounded by Edgar, we may have forgotten Cordelia and her father. But suddenly, 'Enter one with a bloudie knife,' crying 'Help, help! O help!' (V 3 221) who answers Edgar's 'What means this bloody knife?' by

'Tis hot, it smokes;
It comes even from the heart of—O, she's dead!

Surely we must think, for a moment, the victim Cordelia, rather than Goneril?

Kent reminds Albany to ask,

Speak, Edmund; where's the king and where Cordelia?

but again we are left in suspense, for the stage direction has 'Gonerill and Regan's bodies brought out', a slow business. When at last Edmund, repenting, tries to send a reprieve, there is still bustle and muddle.

Perhaps Shakespeare wanted to make the final blow more crushing by introducing what Romeo says happens to condemned men—'a lightning before death' (*Romeo and Juliet* V 3 90). Romeo himself has a moment of joy at Mantua just before he hears of Juliet's death; Antony has one brief victory just before his final defeat; Hamlet jests in the churchyard just before the play starts on its final plunge.

We as audience must be hoping that the reprieve will come in time, and praying with Albany 'The gods defend her!' (V 3 255); but then the final blow falls—*Enter Lear with Cordelia in his arms*—

She's gone for ever. (V 3 259)

We realise that this is so; but twice more Lear himself has hope—

This feather stirs—she lives! (V 3 265)

And the great critic Bradley has suggested that although the audience knows that Cordelia is indeed dead, Lear's last words

Do you see this? Look on her! Look—her lips!
Look there, look there! (V 3 310)

suggest that he thinks the feather stirs and that Cordelia breathes, so that in the end Lear dies of joy.

Questions:

1. Do you agree that the audience may, consciously or subconsciously, remember the earlier occasions when kneeling took place, and connect it with Lear's words (V 3 10)? Or do you think this too far-fetched an idea?
2. Do you agree with Bradley that Lear dies of *joy*?

4. *Tate's version of King Lear*.

It was not only the physical shape of the theatre that changed after the Restoration. Another change of fashion in the theatre led to other major changes in the play. After 1660 female parts were usually played by women. Cordelia was no longer, as in Shakespeare's time, acted by a boy, but by a leading actress, who demanded a part in which she could exhibit her femininity. So Nahum Tate (modestly and nervously, as we can see from his preface, but very firmly) rewrote *King Lear*, adding a love story to 'rectifie', as he explained, 'what was wanting in the Regularity and Probability of the Tale', and 'making the Tale conclude in a Success to the innocent distrest Persons'.

His Cordelia loves Edgar from the beginning, and after all the changes and chances of fortune are over they are united to reign over the kingdom.

The idea of *King Lear* with the conventional ending of the novelette or 'romantic comic', fading out on an embrace, seems strange to us; but let Dr. Johnson in 1765 speak for a hundred and fifty years of play-goers:

> 'The public has decided. Cordelia, from the time of *Tate*, has always retired with victory and felicity. . . . I might relate that I was many years ago so shocked by Cordelia's death, that I know not whether I ever endured to read again the last scenes of the play until I undertook to revise them as an editor.'

Yet another alteration to Shakespeare's *King Lear* was the omission of the Fool's part. The eighteenth century, concerned that Tragedy should be entirely tragic, and Comedy comic, saw no point in his 'babblings'; 'such a character in a Tragedy would not be endured on the modern stage', said George Colman in 1768.

In 1838 Macready the actor-manager, piously striving to restore Shakespeare's text, considered replacing the Fool's part, with its 'terrible contrasts'. 'I described,' writes Macready, 'the sort of fragile, hectic, beautiful-faced, half-idiot-looking boy that he should be. It could never be acted. Bartley observed that a woman should play it. I caught at the idea, and instantly exclaimed, "Miss P. Horton is the very person".' So the first Fool for a hundred and fifty years was a woman, who played with what *John Bull* described as 'deep feeling . . . mingled with archness and pathos'.

Nowadays many of the great actors who have played Lear—Gielgud in 1952, Redgrave in 1953, Laughton in 1959, Schofield in 1962—regard the Fool as so essential to the meaning of the play that when photographed in the part of Lear they have the Fool clinging to them, crouched beside them, integrated with the king.

Let us next consider the character of Lear, and then discuss the function of the Fool.

Questions:

1. Dr. Johnson says that Cordelia's death is 'contrary to the natural ideas of justice, to the hope of the reader, and, what is more strange, to the faith of the Chronicles.' Do you agree? Is there any reason why *King Lear* should not have a 'happy ending'?

2. Discussing his version of *King Lear* in 1768, Colman says, 'The utter improbability of Gloster's imagining, though blind, that he leaped down Dover Cliff, has been justly censured by Doctor Warton; and in the representation [performance on the stage] it is still more liable to objection than in print; I have therefore without scruple omitted it.' Would you omit this scene (or any other) if you were producing *King Lear*? Explain why you would include or exclude it.

3. Admittedly each generation must read and act Shakespeare in its own way. But do you feel that any argument could justify what must be the most extraordinary version of the play ever attempted, the *Queen Lear* performed in New York in 1951? 'The leading lady sonorously described herself', writes Kenneth Tynan, 'as "a very foolish fond old woman" . . . the Fool addressed her throughout as "Auntie" instead of "Nuncle".'

4. It is clear that much which we can gain from a close study of the text is lost in watching a stage performance. What do you feel is gained?

LEAR AND THE FOOL

1. *King Lear*

The central figure of the play from beginning to end is Lear himself. Lear when abandoned is so pathetic a figure that the audience's sympathy goes out to this poor, misused old man so cruelly treated by his daughters, and he is taken at his own valuation: 'so kind a father' (I 5 33); 'I gave you all' (II 4 24);

> . . . a poor old man
> As full of grief as age, wretched in both. (II 4 268–9)
> A poor, infirm, weak and despised old man. (III 2 20)
> . . . I am a man
> More sinned against than sinning. (III 2 59–60)
> Your kind old father whose frank heart gave all.
> (III 4 20)

But as Regan points out, Lear 'hath ever but slenderly known himself' (I 1 290), and if we look dispassionately at the first scene of the play we see a far from admirable figure. Lear lacks what Malcolm in *Macbeth* calls 'the king-becoming graces', that is, the attributes a king ought to possess,

> As justice, verity, temperance, stableness,
> Bounty, perseverance, mercy, lowliness,
> Devotion, patience, courage, fortitude.
> (*Macbeth* IV 3 91)

Lear himself declares that 'the marks of sovereignty' are 'knowledge and reason' (I 4 232) but he exhibits neither of these qualities.

There was much talk in the seventeenth century about the internal struggle a man might undergo between passion (sometimes called 'will', including impulse, desire, lust) and reason. Fulke Greville wrote that

> Passion and Reason self-division cause;

Milton believed that

> Reason in man obscured, or not obeyed,
> Immediately inordinate desires
> And upstart passions catch the government
> From Reason.

Shakespeare often dramatises this struggle. Troilus knows and discusses it: 'Within my soul there doth conduce a fight', and he also speaks of the struggle between 'will and judgement'. (*Troilus and Cressida* V 2 142–147 and II 2 61–67). In *Antony and Cleopatra* it is Enobarbus who sees Antony's fault; he

> would make his will
> Lord of his reason— (III 13 3)

and therefore he lost everything.

It is possible to see Lear's behaviour in the same terms. His emotions over-rule his reason. Vain, arrogant and tyrannical, he stages a theatrical test, so that he may bask in public professions of love by his daughters. It is pure farce, for Gloucester (I 1 3) and Burgundy (I 1 241) know that the kingdom has already been divided, with equal shares for Goneril and Regan, and 'a third more opulent' (I 1 85) (as Lear himself says) for Cordelia. Thwarted by Cordelia in his longing for public adulation, Lear loses all control of his emotions, rants and storms, refuses advice, and banishes the only child who truly loves him. Properly and 'naturally' Lear should be worthy of respect as king, as father and as an old man. He forfeits respect in all three capacities—'Thou should'st not have been old till thou had'st been wise' (I 5 43) says the Fool.

At the beginning of the play Lear is seen as supremely powerful. 'Come not between the dragon and his wrath'

(I 1 121) he cries. Indeed he often seems to claim supernatural powers, particularly when he curses Goneril, taking to himself the destructive forces of nature and threatening with sterility first Goneril (I 4 275) and then the whole world. (III 2 89).

Lear has pretended that he is resigning his reponsibilities through weariness, has declared that he will now 'unburdened crawl toward death' (I 1 40); but it is made quite clear when next we see him that Lear is as autocratic as ever, and is treating Goneril's house as his own (I 3). He is full of vigour, fresh from hunting, shouting for his dinner (I 4 8), his fool and his daughter (I 4 43–51) in the old imperious way. Goneril is infuriated by this

> idle old man
> That still would manage these authorities
> That he hath given away. (I 3 17)

But the habit of command, and the expectation of admiration, when both have been established in youth (IV 4 96) are not easily given up. As the disguised Kent says, Lear still has 'authority' in his countenance (I 4 28, 31); *that* he cannot give away.

Se we are shown that Lear has tried to abandon his responsibilities while yet retaining his power, and this is against the natural order. For though a subject obeyed his king, as a servant his master, as a child his father, yet king, master and father must be in turn responsible for the welfare of subject, servant and child. When defied both as king and as father, Lear is astounded, bewildered. He tries to meet the situation with simple irony, and pretends not to recognise this brawling woman, asking Goneril, 'Are you our daughter?' (I 4 219) and 'Your name, fair gentlewoman?' (I 4 236) Goneril both rebukes and threatens him, so Lear breaks into ravings and curses

(I 4 276 ff.) with an extravagance and wildness far greater than that shown in his cursing of Cordelia (I 1 108). When he turns for comfort to Regan, he is again bewildered as well as enraged. He finds his messenger in the stocks (II 4), his daughter and her husband at first refusing him, their 'king' and 'dear father' an audience (II 4 85 ff.) and then defending Goneril's behaviour (II 4 137) and indeed telling him to ask her forgiveness (II 4 146–8).

The world indeed seems upside down, and he symbolises this by pretending to kneel to his daughter, to shock her into realisation of the situation. But Regan is not shocked even by this total reversal of correct behaviour, this total lack of 'decorum', or fittingness; she is merely embarrassed and annoyed by Lear's 'unsightly tricks' (II 4 153).

Cursing Goneril, Lear still tries to cling to the idea that Regan feels, and will behave, differently, that she at least is still his daughter. Goneril's eyes, he says,

> are fierce; but thine
> Do comfort and not burn. (II 4 168)

Lear now appeals, but in vain, to

> The offices of nature, bond of childhood,
> Effects of courtesy, dues of gratitude. (II 4 174)

He even reminds Regan (in a phrase reminiscent of the bond of the marriage service) of 'thy half o' th'kingdom', 'wherein I thee endowed'. But his two elder daughters unite against him, and it never occurs to Lear that it was he himself who, by casting out Cordelia, first broke the sacred bond between father and child, and set an example of enmity and discord within the family.

When Goneril and Regan coolly calculate how many knights Lear really needs (II 4 225–260)—a hundred?

fifty? twenty-five? ten? 'What needs one?'—we remember that they are following their father's example: it was he who first made love and generosity things to be calculated and measured. When Lear cries out 'O reason not the need' (II 4 260), this is more than his agonised recognition that calculation is no way to approach human relationships. In the following speech he relates his own case to a beggar's; for the first time he seems to feel that he may be in some sense an ordinary man. Shakespeare has prepared us, dramatically, by Lear's earlier declaration that rather than return to Goneril he will

> abjure all roofs, and choose
> To wage against *the enmity o' th' air*,
> To be a comrade with the wolf and owl— (II 4 204)

echoing what we have just heard from the disguised Edgar.

In the immediately preceding scene we have been shown Edgar as a naked beggar, declaring that he will

> with presented nakedness outface
> *The winds and persecutions of the sky*. (II 3 11)

He will be a Tom o' Bedlam, a madman,

> the *basest* and most poorest shape
> That ever penury in contempt of *man*
> *Brought near to beast*. (II 3 7)

And these are the words and images fresh in the minds of the audience when Lear bursts forth:

> O reason not the *need*. Our *basest beggars*
> Are in the poorest things superfluous.
> Allow not *nature* more than *nature needs*,
> *Man's life is cheap as beast's*. Thou art a lady;
> If only to go warm were gorgeous,
> Why, *nature needs* not what thou gorgeous wear'st,
> Which scarcely keeps thee warm. But for true *need*—

You heavens, give me patience—patience I *need!*

(II 4 260)

Man, if supplied only with the barest necessities, merely enough to keep him alive, is no more than a beast. Clothes are worn not only for warmth, but as a sign of civilisation and station, or, as we might say, as status symbols. Nature must be modified by nurture, bringing up, education. This cluster of ideas, drawing on the audience's glimpse of Edgar's condition, and on the main themes of 'nature' and 'degree', is finally completely developed when Lear on the heath, with the naked Edgar at his side, tries to tear off the trappings of civilisation, and declares that 'unaccommodated man' is 'no more but such a poor, bare, forked animal as thou art'.

(III 4 101–9)

When facing his two mean and calculating daughters, and trying to hammer home by repetition the idea that to give only what 'nature needs' is not enough, Lear is so far reasonable, maintaining an argument. But his reason is overcome by passion, he appeals to the heavens, and when he rails at his daughters as 'unnatural hags' (II 4 274) the broken rhythm of his speech matches the tumult of his feelings, and the feeble, choked incoherence of his impotent threats.

No, you unnatural hags,
I will have such revenges on you both
That all the world shall—I will do such things—
What they are yet I know not, but they shall be
The terrors of the earth! (II 4 274)

Lear feels his reason going:

O Fool, I shall go mad! (II 4 282)

When after this last outburst Lear is shut out from the castle, to the ominous sound of thunder (one of the original stage directions) his mind is indeed tottering. He

> Strives in his little world of man to out-storm
> The to-and-fro conflicting wind and rain,
> (III 1 10)

but as he later admits, he finds that his power has limits:

> The thunder would not peace at my bidding . . . I am not ague-proof. (IV 6 102, 105)

He suffers from dizziness, which was thought an actual symptom of madness or mental unbalance—'My wits begin to turn' (III 2 67). And in the double storm, within and without, in the extreme of misery, Lear for the first time notices someone else's actual plight. It is to the Fool that he turns, the Fool who has loyally followed him into the wilderness.

> Come on, my boy. How dost, my boy? Art cold?
> . . .
> Poor fool and knave, I have one part in my heart
> That's sorry yet for thee. (III 2 68, 72)

When eventually some crude shelter is reached, again Lear thinks of the Fool and bids him 'In, boy, go first'. (III 4 26) Though he still feels that his daughters' behaviour is entirely unprovoked (III 4 19–20), Lear at last seems to realise that others may be suffering as well as himself, in fact, that such suffering may be common. And he feels his neglected responsibility:

> Poor naked wretches, wheresoe'er you are,
> That bide the pelting of this pitiless storm,
> How shall your houseless heads and unfed sides,
> Your looped and windowed raggedness, defend you
> From seasons such as these? O, I have ta'en
> Too little care of this! (III 4 28)

Always sure that he was a king, concerned for himself

alone, Lear has been so self-absorbed that he has forgotten that he is also a man, and that he is responsible for other men who exist and suffer. Shakespeare had made Henry V argue that

> The king is but a man . . . all his senses have but human conditions: his *ceremonies* laid by, in his *nakedness* he appears but a *man* (*Henry V* IV 1 106)

And now when Lear does 'expose' himself 'to feel what wretches feel' (III 4 34) he learns from naked Edgar what '*unaccommodated man*' is (III 4 106). And it is this naked man that Lear hails as his 'philosopher', 'noble philosopher', 'good Athenian' (III 4 154, 173, 175, 180).

Shakespeare next confronts Lear, the king spiritually blinded by his arrogance and passion, with Gloucester, the courtier physically blinded because he too put his trust in the wrong child, the child born of his father's error. When Gloucester asks, 'Is't not the king?' (IV 6 107), Lear, though mad, claims 'Ay, every inch a king'; but when Gloucester would kiss his hand Lear says 'Let me wipe it first; it smells of mortality' (IV 6 133)—he acknowledges that he is also a man, a mere mortal man.

Lear has lost his reason, and so has lost control of the animal impulses which were thought to be part of every man. In the great chain of being, each order contained the qualities of all orders below it. Stones existed; vegetables existed and also grew, so possessed the 'vegetable soul'; animals existed and grew, and also had senses, so possessed both 'vegetable' and 'sensible' souls; man existed and grew and had senses, but as well, in order to control his animal impulses and in order to communicate with God, had the gift of reason and possessed not only a 'vegetable' and a 'sensible' but also a 'rational' soul. Lear has lost his rational soul. So he dwells on lust, seeing man as a battleground between the spirit and the flesh:

> But to the girdle do the gods inherit,
> Beneath is all the fiends. (IV 6 106)

The whole of Lear's speech (IV 6 108–131) exhibits one particular facet of the disordered, topsy-turvy world he now inhabits. Properly, marriage should be part of the orderly scheme of life, yet how can adultery be condemned, if marriage produces Goneril and Regan, and adultery Edmund? For Lear still believes Edmund to be 'kinder to his father', closer kindred, more loving,

> than my daughters
> Got 'tween the lawful sheets. (IV 6 115)

Virtuous love-making within the marriage bond must give way to promiscuity. All is hypocrisy: the apparently refined and genteel court lady, who is shocked even to hear sex mentioned, who appears so sexually frigid, is in fact an eager whore, an animal. And Lear falls into vituperation of the sexual parts worthy of the early Fathers of the Church:

> There's hell, there's darkness, there is the sulphurous pit;
> Burning, scalding, stench, consumption: fie, fie, fie, pah, pah!

We should note, I think, that the disgust expressed by Lear, by Leontes (*Winters Tale* 1 2 passim) and by Prospero (*Tempest* IV 1 15–30) is not directed at the sexual act, but at the adulterous act. This is quite distinct from Lear's reproof to the beadle (IV 6 159–163) for his hypocrisy, or Lear's desire to flatten and to annihilate the whole world, expressed when he begs the thunder

> Crack Nature's moulds, all germens spill at once
> That make ingrateful man. (III 2 8)

It is Timon who, bidding 'matrons, turn incontinent!' (IV 1 3), telling the maid that 'Thy mistress is o' the brothel' (IV 1 13) and speaking of 'the counterfeit matron' who is in fact like Lear's 'dame', 'a bawd' (IV 3 113–5), goes on to imagine that venereal disease can be used to wipe out 'all':

> plague all,
> That your activity may defeat and quell
> The source of all erection (*Timon* IV 3 163)

Timon is sickened because riches, not virtues, command respect—

> the learned pate
> Ducks to the golden fool. (IV 3 17)

And now, when Lear is apparently completely mad, he too recognises the hollowness of outward authority lacking inner virtue—'a dog's obeyed in office' (IV 6 158) —and the falsity of judging by outward appearance:

> Through tattered clothes small vices do appear:
> Robes and furred gowns hide all. (IV 6 163)

We are prepared for Cordelia's return and for Lear's rescue when a Gentleman, shocked by Lear's madness, exclaims:

> Thou hast one daughter
> Who *redeems nature* from the general curse
> Which twain have brought her to. (IV 6 203)

And when Cordelia meets her stricken father, for the first time since she was banished, she prays that 'this great breach in his abused nature' be cured. Nature, to be healthy, must be harmonious; Lear's senses are 'untuned and jarring', but can be healed by music. (IV 7 15–16 and 25) Music, says Richard II, 'Have holp madmen to their wits' (V 5 62), and we remember the healing use of music in modern mental hospitals, as well as David playing to Saul.

We find constant religious allusion. Cordelia, who 'redeems nature' (IV 6 202), compares this return of her prodigal father with that of the Prodigal Son (IV 7 39–40). Lear speaks as if he were Lazarus:

> You do me wrong to take me out o'th'grave.
> (IV 7 45)

It is a scene of the most tender restoration and redemption written with complete and moving simplicity of language. Lear, who has condemned the 'plainness' of Cordelia (I 1 128) now manages 'to deal plainly' himself (IV 7 62).

When the reunited Lear and Cordelia are captured by Edmund, Lear is finally reconciled not only to Cordelia but to his fate: now he kneels in all sincerity to a daughter:

> When thou dost ask me blessing, I'll kneel down
> And ask of thee forgiveness. (V 3 10)

Their final rescue comes too late. Cordelia has been hanged. In a last upsurge of spirit, Lear's great strength is renewed; once more 'the dragon' (I 1 121) he cries to the dead Cordelia:

> I killed the knave that was a-hanging thee.
> (V 3 274)

Lear cannot now concentrate; he manages to recognise Kent but 'he knows not what he says' (V 3 293). All that matters is Cordelia, and she is hanged. 'No, no, no life' (V 3 305).

But when he turns to her body, he fancies that the feather on her lips stirs, and that she lives. He is overcome by rapture, and, like Gloucester's,

> . . . his flawed heart
> (Alack too weak the conflict to support)
> 'Twixt two extremes of passion, joy and grief,
> Burst smilingly. (V 3 195)

Lear and Cordelia, separated by their common pride

despite their mutual love, are finally reunited, and Kent speaks for us all:

> Vex not his ghost: O let him pass; he hates him
> That would upon the rack of this tough world
> Stretch him out longer. (V 3 313)

Further Reading:

A. C. Bradley, *King Lear* in *Shakespearean Tragedy* (A landmark in criticism, though this kind of discussion of character is no longer fashionable).

H. Granville-Barker, *King Lear* (section *The Characters and their Interplay*) in *Prefaces to Shakespeare First Series*. (Discussion from the point of view of an actor and producer, showing that *King Lear* 'is directed to one end; the play's acting in a theatre'.)

Questions:

1. We have been discussing Lear's shortcomings: what were his virtues, if any? If Lear's opponents were not so unpleasant, would we have any sympathy with him?

2. This might be described as a tragedy about a man whose passions overmastered his reason. Do you know of any other comparable Shakespearean characters? Compare, for instance, Antony (in *Antony and Cleopatra*), Hotspur, Troilus or Othello.

3. If you have read other plays in which Shakespeare shows the relationship of father and daughter, compare, say, Capulet and Juliet, or Prospero and Miranda, or Polonius and Ophelia, with Lear and his daughters.

4. Critics talk of Lear being 'educated' or 'enlightened'. What were the things that contributed to this process? What did he learn?

2. *The Fool*

To modern audiences the Fool seems an outlandish kind of person. But the figure of the Fool was familiar to Shakespeare's original audience, in two connections. As a stock character on the stage, he linked actors and audience, playing tricks on the persons in the play, and commenting directly to the audience. But also, as the traditional court jester, the Fool was a privileged person in the royal household who, as Jaques says in *As You Like It* (II 7 49) could 'blow on' whom he pleased —that is, could comment with some freedom on the stupid behaviour of his betters. Touched too closely by his 'jests', Goneril indignantly calls Lear's Fool 'all-licensed' (I 4 201), and also 'more knave than fool' (I 4 315). In *Twelfth Night*, however, another great lady (Olivia) declares that 'there is no slander in an allowed fool, though he do nothing but rail' (I 5 100), and later Viola reminds us that a Fool could not afford to be foolish:

> This fellow's wise enough to play the fool,
> And to do that well craves a kind of wit . . .
> . . . this is a practice
> As full of labour as a wise man's art. (III 1 68)

Lear's Fool seems to have studied his art—many of the questions he asks Lear (I 5 17–38) occur in a popular Elizabethan book, the *Book of Sidrach or The Sapience of Nature*, which consists of questions and answers on 'reasons of nature'. The book was supposed to have been compiled by Sidrach, 'philosopher' to King Boctris of Armenia—kings traditionally kept a philosopher at hand to answer tricky questions and to advise them generally. We may note that in *King Lear* the roles are reversed—the fool questions the king instead of the king the philosopher. But when later Lear finds in the naked Tom o'

Bedlam, the disguised Edgar, a 'philosopher', Lear does question him about 'reasons of nature'—a stock question, 'What is the cause of thunder?' (III 4 155) and then a very personal question—about Regan: 'Is there any cause in nature that makes these hard hearts?' (III 6 76).

Perhaps Jaques foreshadows the remedial purpose of Lear's Fool when he exclaims:

> Invest me in my motley; give me leave
> To speak my mind, and I will through and through
> Cleanse the foul body of th'infected world
> If they will *patiently* receive my medicine.
>
> (*As You Like It* II 7 58)

We have seen that the need for patience is a recurring theme in *King Lear*.

Lear seems more sensitive in his relations with his Fool than with his daughters. When he goes to stay with Goneril, he does not at first particularly notice her neglect of himself and his knights (I 4 64); he does notice that the Fool, who like himself loves Cordelia, misses her and pines in her absence (I 4 74–7).

Lear's Fool is not without worldly wisdom. He realises what is happening to the king while Lear is still entirely oblivious of his loss of power. (I 4 100–188) When the disguised Kent seeks service with the fallen Lear, the Fool offers Kent his coxcomb, the badge of a fool, 'for taking one's part that's out of favour' (I 4 100). But when Lear is actually turned out by Goneril, the Fool (like Kent) forgets self-interest; 'Tarry, take the Fool with thee' (I 4 319) he says, and later he sings:

> But I will tarry; the Fool will stay
> And let the wise man fly. (II 4 79)

The deflating commonsense of the Fool contrasts

with Edgar's assumed madness and adds grotesque comedy to Lear's ravings.

> *Lear*: What, has his daughters brought him to this pass? Could'st thou save nothing? Would'st thou give 'em all?
>
> *Fool*: Nay, he reserved a blanket; else we had all been shamed. (III 4 62)

Again, when Lear tries to tear off his clothes, to become like Edgar a 'poor, bare, forked animal', again the Fool deflates him: 'Prithee, nuncle, be contented; 'tis a naughty night to swim in' (III 4 110).

What critics have described as 'the fool's droll or pitiful babblings', his 'tasteless jokes', are often in reality shrewd comments on the action. The Fool sums up the whole position—'Thou should'st not have been old till thou had'st been wise' (I 5 43). 'This is not altogether fool', (I 4 152) says Kent, and he is right. The Fool is a mirror, striving to show Lear his true image. There are, says the Fool, two fools:

> The one in motley here *(pointing to himself)*
> The other found out—there! *(pointing to Lear)*
>
> *Lear*: Dost thou call me fool, boy?
>
> *Fool*: All thy other titles thou hast given away; that thou wast born with. (I 4 147)

And he laments

> That such a king should play bo-peep
> And go the fools among. (I 4 177)

It is the Fool alone who from the first sees the true nature and extent of Lear's folly. 'May not an ass know when the cart draws the horse?' (I 4 224) He sums up Lear's mistake: 'Thou mad'st thy daughters thy mothers' (I 4 172). The reversal of proper natural order is crudely emphasised: 'Thou gav'st them the rod and putt'st down thine own breeches' (I 4 173). Like the hedge sparrow in the song, sings the Fool, Lear has had 'it head bit off by it young', and the result is, 'So out went the candle and we were left darkling' (I 4 17)—Lear's abdication leaves the kingdom without the light of good government.

In the first scene of the play, Lear has described Cordelia's fortune: 'Nothing will come of nothing' (I 1 89). Now the Fool asks Lear in his turn:

> Can you make no use of nothing, nuncle? (I 4 131)

And Lear unwittingly describes his own fortunes:

> Why no, boy, nothing can be made out of nothing. (I 4 133)

Again and again the speeches of the Fool reflect Lear's actions in their true light. But when Lear's 'wits are gone' (III 6 86) and, drawing imaginary bed-curtains round him, he retreats from the sane world—'So, so; we'll go to supper i'th'morning' (III 6 83)—the Fool echoes his master's paradox, and vanishes from the play—'I'll go to bed at noon' (III 6 84). His function is over.

Lear, while still absolutely arrogant, has said casually to the Fool, 'No, lad, teach me' (I 4 40). It is bitterly ironical that he is, in fact, absolutely deaf to the Fool's teaching and warning. 'Who is it that can tell me who I am?' cries Lear. The Fool answers, 'Lear's shadow' (I 4 230), that is, Lear's image, himself; but the king is oblivious. Nevertheless Lear's affection for the Fool is clear—'my pretty knave' (I 4 97), 'my boy' (I 4 107),—and is unmistakably declared when he describes the beloved dead Cordelia as 'poor fool' (V 3 305).

Further Reading:

H. Granville Barker, *Prefaces to Shakespeare First Series*—the section on *The Fool* in *King Lear*.

Questions:

1. For what reasons do you consider the part of the Fool either (a) useless or (b) useful or (c) essential to the play *King Lear*?

2. Critics have described the Fool as Lear's guardian angel, as Lear's conscience, and as the voice of common-sense. Do you accept any of these definitions? Can you provide another definition of his function in the play?

3. The critic Frank Kermode commented that in Peter Brook's 1964 production of *King Lear* the Fool is 'a sage-fool, intelligent, and doing his foolery as a professional act'. Is this a satisfactory way to play the part? Would you prefer Macready's 'fragile, hectic, beautiful-faced, half-idiot-looking boy'? How do you picture the Fool?

CORDELIA AND HER SISTERS

The tiny, low-voiced figure of Cordelia,* though she appears in only four of the scenes, and speaks only 112 lines, is of the highest importance. Cordelia has been described by various critics as a 'Christ-like figure', as symbolic of 'the highest moral rectitude', even as 'Nature herself'. And in the play France, talking of Cordelia, certainly uses words with theological overtones, 'believe', 'faith', 'reason', 'miracle' (I 1 221) while Cordelia's own language recalls St. Luke's account of Christ in the Temple—

O dear father,
It is thy business that I go about! (IV 4 23)

Lear, recovering from madness, hails her as resurrecting him from the grave, and as 'a soul in bliss', 'a spirit' (IV 7 45, 46, 49). Cordelia's Gentleman describes how

she shook
The *holy* water from her *heavenly* eyes, (IV 3 31)

and later declares that Cordelia '*redeems* nature from the general curse' (IV 6 204); Kent too describes her as 'seeking to give losses their remedies' (II 2 166). All this may suggest a distinction not only between kind and unkind daughters, good and bad children, but between the forces of light and darkness, good and evil.

Cordelia typifies 'kindness' in both senses, for even in the first scene of the play she loves her father as nature would enjoin, 'according to my bond' (I 1 92)—to her this bond is not a mere legal pact, but the sacred tie between father and child. The strength and importance

* 'tiny': 'our last and least' (I 1 82) and Lear can carry her in his arms. 'low-voiced': see I 1 153 and V 3 273.

of this natural tie is brought out in earlier versions of the story. Cordell, in *A Mirour for Magistrates* (1586), tells her father Leire:

> For nature so doth bind and duty me compel
> To love you, as I ought my father, well.

In Spenser's version of the story (*Faery Queene* Bk II Canto x stanza 27, (1590)) after Gonorill does 'protest' and Regan has 'profest' their great loves, Cordell simply 'said she loved him, *as behoov'd*': and this is what Shakespeare makes his Cordelia say:

> You have begot me, bred me, loved me. I
> Return those duties back *as are right fit*,
> Obey you, love you and most honour you. (I 1 195)

By the end of the play Cordelia goes much further than mere duty requires, and in pure love rescues and restores the stricken Lear.

Shakespeare's Cordelia is above all straightforward and honest; she combines sweetness with strength, and we find these qualities in another of her forerunners, Cordella in the older play of *King Leir*, shown both in speech and action. She is wooed by the Gallian king, disguised as a palmer, who pretends that he has been sent by his master, the Gallian king, to ask for her hand. Cordella prefers the palmer—'seek for thyself to woo'—and when he doubts if she can endure a palmer's poverty, a life 'full of penury', she replies:

> O yes, I can, and happy if I might:
> I'll hold thy palmer's staff within my hand,
> And think it is the sceptre of a queen.
> Sometime I'll set thy bonnet on my head,
> And think I wear a rich imperial crown.
> Sometime I'll help thee in thy holy prayers,
> And think I am with thee in Paradise.

> Thus I'll mock fortune, as she mocketh me,
> And never will my lovely choice repent:
> For having thee, I shall have all content.

Cordella is frank, simple, loving, but firm; so is Cordelia.

As in the morality plays a character on entering usually assists the audience by announcing his name and nature, so in the same way the first speech of many of Shakespeare's creations strikes the keynote of the character. Shylock, for instance, says 'Three thousand ducats, well?' (*Merchant of Venice* I 3 1); Cleopatra, 'If it be love indeed, tell me how much' (*Antony and Cleopatra* I 1 14); Sir Toby Belch, 'What a plague means my niece to take the death of her brother thus? I am sure care's an enemy to life' (*Twelfth Night* I 3 1). And Cordelia's first line is,

> What shall Cordelia speak? Love, and be silent.
> (I 1 61)

She will not, perhaps she cannot, gush. Unlike Hamlet she cannot 'unpack her heart with words' (II 2 622). For Cordelia is, like her father, proud and independent. She will not pander to his vanity by telling him he will have all her love, even when she marries. Her strong common-sense—and perhaps some sense of the ridiculous—asks:

> Why have my sisters husbands, if they say
> They love you all? Haply, when I shall wed,
> That lord whose hand must take my plight shall carry
> Half my love with him, half my care and duty.
> Sure I shall never marry like my sisters,
> To love my father all. (I 1 98)

She matches her father's obstinacy:

> *Lear*: . . . What can you say to draw
> A third more opulent than your sisters? Speak.
> *Cordelia*: Nothing, my lord.

Lear: Nothing?
Cordelia: Nothing.
Lear: Nothing will come of nothing. Speak again.
Cordelia: Unhappy that I am, I cannot heave*
My heart into my mouth. (I 1 84)

'Cannot', or will not? But though she is as firm as her father, there is one great difference. Lear loses control; Cordelia remains, in Kent's words,

a queen
Over her passion, who, most rebel-like
Sought to be king o'er her. (IV 3 14)

When eventually Cordelia returns to rescue Lear, her devotion restores his sanity. The wheel comes full circle: Lear had once dismissed her 'without our grace, our love, our benison'. (I 1 264) Now when she begs,

O look upon me, sir,
And hold your hand in benediction o'er me,
(IV 7 57)

it is Lear who attempts to kneel to her. Kent has accused Lear of madness in banishing Cordelia (I 1 145) and now Lear himself admits his state and calls himself 'a very foolish fond old man'—'I fear I am not in my rightful mind' (IV 7 60, 63).

When they are captured and about to be sent to prison, Lear is content to go. But Cordelia, though her grief is for her father's humiliation rather than for her own, yet wishes to face her conquerors: the last words we hear her speak are as firm and dignified as the first:

Shall we not see these daughters and these sisters?
(V 3 7)

* heave: notice the word Cordelia uses, with its distasteful suggestions of physical sickness; it emphasises her disgust at the proceedings.

Cordelia has never been deceived by the 'professed bosoms' (I 1 270) of Goneril and Regan. Their 'large speeches' (I 1 183) and fulsome protestations (I 1 34–60 and 67–75) ring false and sound cheap when compared with Cordelia's dignified statements of her faith and her integrity. (I 1 94–103 and 229–231).

As soon as Goneril and Regan are alone together they drop into familiar prose: there are no pretences between them. They freely discuss the flaws in their father's character—'He hath *ever* but slenderly known himself' (I 1 290), says Regan in a key phrase—he has *always* been unable to examine his own motives, to see himself clearly. 'The best and soundest of his time hath been but rash' (I 1 292) says Goneril, echoing her namesake Gonorill in the old play, 'For he, you know, is always in extremes'—a vivid description of Shakespeare's Lear too. Goneril and Regan fully realise Lear's 'poor judgement' (I 1 288) in casting off the only daughter who cares for him; but they have no pity for him, only scorn.

Goneril is without shame, and will use any means for her ends. She will even conspire with a servant, and egg him on to enrage her father—

> Put on what weary negligence you please—
>
> (I 3 13)

so that she can have further cause for complaint.

Each daughter in turn speaks to her father in the tone a scolding teacher might use to a tiresome child.

> Put away
> These dispositions which of late transport you
> From what you rightly are— (I 4 221)

as it were 'I don't know what's got into you lately'—says Goneril; and she speaks of his 'new pranks' with severity and a hint of power in reserve:

Be then desired
By her that else will take the thing she begs.(I 4 247)

There is a kind of coarseness about this, as if she were a harassed mother crying 'Do what I tell you, or I'll slap you', and Lear's protests affect her no more than the helpless wailings of a child. Her husband is appalled by Lear's curses, but Goneril shakes them off unheedingly. (I 4 291–4).

Regan's equally cold replies to Lear's impassioned pleas for help prepare us for the scene between the sisters and Cornwall after Lear is turned out of Gloucester's castle. (II 4 283 ff.) We have been carried along by Lear's growing emotion, so that when he has stormed out it is like a douche of cold water to hear the matter-of-fact talk of Cornwall, Goneril and Regan as they justify, on grounds merely of practical convenience, their behaviour.

Cornwell: Let us withdraw; 'twill be a storm.
Regan: This house is little: the old man and's people
Cannot be well bestowed.
Goneril: 'Tis his own blame; hath put himself from rest
And needs must taste his folly. . . . (II 4 283)

Regan too indulges in this cool, smug, moralising:

O sir, to wilful men
The injuries that they themselves procure
Must be their schoolmasters. (II 4 298)

This continual self-justification can be more repugnant than any display of rage: but it is not unlike Lear's early uncritical view of his own behaviour.

Critics have protested that the blinding of Gloucester is too horrible a scene to be acted. But the light thrown by it on Goneril (who first suggests, 'Pluck out his eyes'

(III 7 5)) and on Regan is more horrifying than the physical cruelty of Cornwall. What sort of 'hard heart' can watch an old man's eye plucked out and cry only 'Th'other too' (III 7 70)? And when he is blinded, make a grotesque, and truly a 'sick' joke—'let him smell his way to Dover' (III 7 93)? And when Regan later regrets that Gloucester was not killed outright, it is not this cruelty that she regrets, but—again for practical reasons —their 'ignorance' of public reaction to their behaviour:

> where he arrives he moves
> All hearts against us. (IV 4 10)

And she explains in the same breath that Edmund has gone off to kill Gloucester 'in pity of his misery' (as people speak of putting an animal out of pain) and also

> to descry
> The strength o'th'enemy. (IV 5 11 ff.)

Goneril and Regan seem to represent pure evil. They do not even remain loyal to one another; as soon as they have obtained power, there are rumours of 'likely wars' (II 1 10) between them. They sin against 'nature' not only as daughters, but as sisters (against Cordelia and against each other) and also as wives. Shakespeare shows us by a series of suggestions and hints, with only a few lines of actual love-making (IV 2 17–25), their rivalry over Edmund and their suspicions of each other growing. Edmund is well aware of his power over them, and completely cynical about it:

> Which of them shall I take?
> Both? One? Or neither? Neither can be enjoyed
> If both remain alive. (V 1 57)

Finally, in a scene of grotesque irony, Goneril—knowing that she has already poisoned her sister, and with her husband still alive beside her despite her plans to murder him—has to hear Regan claim Edmund as her new husband.

When her crimes are discovered, Goneril commits suicide; but it is notable that neither she nor Regan feels any sort of remorse for their behaviour, nor even (it seems) any sense that they have done wrong, despite their failure as daughters, as sisters, as wives and lastly, as princesses. Goneril puts herself above her father, her husband, and finally—'most monstrous' (V 3 158)—above the law:

The laws are mine, not thine;
Who can arraign me for't? (V 3 157)

But this is her last cry of pride: being found out, she cannot live. Soon 'The bodies of Goneril and Regan are brought in', as if Shakespeare was determined not only to tell us, but to show us, that the wicked will not flourish for ever.

Questions:

1. 'Cordelia, like her sisters, is in many respects a chip of the old block'. Can you see any likeness to their father in his daughters?

2. 'Shakespeare attempts to show absolute love and goodness, in the person of Cordelia, destroyed by the powers of this world, but the price he pays is that Cordelia, as a dramatic character, is a bore.' Do you agree with W. H. Auden on either point?

3. Stopford Brooks asks us to 'just imagine what these two haughty, high-tempered, icy-minded, very intelligent women had suffered', and to sympathise with Goneril and Regan; can you justify their behaviour towards Lear?

4. Do you, like one critic, find Goneril and Regan 'almost interchangeable'? How would you distinguish between them?

THE SUBPLOT AND THE GLOUCESTER FAMILY

The tale of King Lear and his daughters is told in the *Mirror for Magistrates* (1586) and in the *Faery Queene* (1591), as well as in the older play *King Leir* and in Holinshed's *Chronicle* (1574). In this story and in that of 'the Paphlagonian unkind king' and his sons, from Sidney's *Arcadia*, Shakespeare found two closely parallel plots, which continually echo one another, and seem to show the audience that this is not just the story of one particular family, but of relationships which could occur in any family.

Lear has good and bad daughters, Gloucester good and bad sons; each mistakes the good child for the bad, and vice-versa; the good child is disinherited and rejected in favour of the bad. The plots cross when Lear is condemned by Gloucester's wicked Edmund, and Gloucester reviled by Lear's wicked Regan and Goneril. The good child returns to save the father, who in neither case immediately recognises his saviour. Even in such details as the emphasis on the word 'nothing' in Lear's interrogation of Cordelia (I 1 85) and in Gloucester's interrogation of Edmund (I 2 31) the stories echo each other; again, Lear is urged to 'see better' (I 1 157) and Gloucester needs spectacles (I 2 36).

We have seen how the trials of Lear and Gloucester, the spiritual blindness of the king and the physical blindness of the courtier, their suffering and endurance, run side by side throughout the play, and how Cordelia and Edgar are matched in patience and love. Edgar at the end says to the defeated Edmund who has so deeply injured him, 'Let's exchange charity' (V 3 165). We may think that Cordelia and Edgar are matched also in simplicity and in lack of worldly wisdom. Edgar is

> a brother noble,
> Whose nature is so far from doing harms
> That he suspects none, (I 2 82)

and so falls too easy a victim to Edmund's malice.

Old age was commonly considered venerable: when Lear is defied by his children he calls on the heavens, old themselves, to 'send down and take my part' (II 4 185). But Goneril and Regan feel no respect for mere age, but rather a callous irritation with 'the unruly waywardness that infirm and choleric years bring with them' (I 1 295). 'Old fools are babes again' (I 3 20), says Goneril. Three times she refers to Lear's old age as 'dotage', and when Lear cries with bitter sarcasm 'Age is unnecessary' (II 4 151), he is really precisely defining what his elder daughters—and Edmund—believe.

Edmund echoes this in the letter which he pretends was written by his brother:

> 'This policy and reverence of age makes the world bitter to the best of our times, keeps our fortunes from us till our oldness cannot relish them. I begin to find an idle and fond bondage in the oppression of aged tyranny, who sways, not as it had power, but as it is suffered.' (I 2 47)

Regan's attitude is just the same:

> O sir, you are old . . .
> . . . you should be ruled and led
> By some discretion that discerns your state
> Better than yourself. (II 4 142)

The position of the resentful children is summed up when she says:

I pray you, father, being weak, seem so. (II 4 197)

Edmund gives his own view, though pretending it is Edgar's, when he declares it 'to be fit that, sons at perfect age, and fathers declined, the father should be as ward to the son, and the son manage his revenue' (I 2 74). We are reminded of the law of the jungle, of the wolf-pack whose leader is only leader as long as he is the strongest male in the group; as soon as his energies fail he must be destroyed and replaced. 'The younger rises as the old doth fall' (III 3 24) says Edmund, and the implication is, the sooner the better.

Lear has already, as the Fool points out, made 'his daughters his mothers'; Goneril and Regan have no hesitation in destroying their father in order to have complete enjoyment of 'his revenue'. Edmund too is completely callous in his determination to displace Edgar and to destroy his father: later, in order to get the crown, he plays off Goneril and Regan against each other in the same ruthless and inhuman way, with a kind of joking cynicism.

Edmund is what was called in Shakespeare's time a 'malcontent'. The word bore the same kind of implications that 'red' bears today in the most right-wing conservative circles in England, or in the U.S.A.—someone out to upset the natural order of society. 'Discord to malcontents is very manna', writes Marston in his play *The Malcontent*, and he tells us that a malcontent is 'free as air', that is, he does not feel any obligations either to individuals or to society as a whole. The world is his oyster and he sees no reason why he should not open and swallow it.

Edmund has no real position in the regular ranks of society, because he is a bastard; he has no inheritance to expect; his advancement will come not from any law of natural succession, but only from what he can do for himself:

> Let me, if not by birth, have lands by wit. (I 2 186)

Edmund reminds us of Shakespeare's Richard III, who in the same remorseless way was determined to get personal power, and who regarded those who opposed him or stood between him and the throne as mere obstacles to be removed. Some of Shakespeare's usurpers —Henry IV, Claudius and Macbeth, for instance—feel that they have done wrong in seizing power, and are haunted by a deep sense of guilt. Edmund pursues his confident, self-satisfied way, glorying in his own cleverness, until almost literally his last gasp—

> I pant for life. Some good I mean to do
> Despite of my own *nature*. (V 3 241)

If Cordelia represents 'natural' goodness, perhaps Edmund typifies 'natural' wickedness. And we may wonder how valuable or how sincere this last minute repentance is.

Has Edmund any justification? Coleridge thought Edmund deeply wounded by his father's coarse introduction of him 'in a tone betwixt waggery and shame', and Shakespeare does indicate Gloucester's indifference to Edmund's worldly advancement at court—'He hath been out nine years and away he shall again' (I 1 31). But the real bitterness of Edmund's position is expressed by the piled-up epithets in his first soliloquy:

> Why *bastard*? wherefore *base*?
> Why brand they us
> With *base*? with *baseness*? *bastardy*? *base, base*?
> *Legitimate* Edgar . . .
> . . . *bastard* Edmund

. . . *legitimate*. Fine word, *Legitimate*!
Well, my *legitimate* . . .
Edmund the *base*
Shall top th'*legitimate* . . .
Now, gods, stand up for *bastards*! (I 2 6 ff.)

Some modern critics, fashionably anxious to find excuses for the underdog, attempt to justify Edmund's behaviour: his bastardy, after all, was not his fault. And some modern producers have Edmund acted with such dash and swagger and vitality, that in this play where no one else seems to be enjoying life at all, the audience find him a rather sympathetic character. But I think that to Shakespeare Edmund was a particularly nasty specimen of a malcontent, or 'machiavel'—so called because Machiavelli's book on government, *The Prince* (1513), was thought to advocate the unscrupulous pursuit of political power. And Edmund's rebellion against authority was, as Edwin Muir has pointed out, the same sin as that of Lucifer, when he rebelled against God and was cast out of heaven.

You may have noticed that in mediaeval pictures of the Last Judgement, the pictures of hell and the wicked are usually much more interesting, and certainly livelier, than the pictures of heaven and the good. And we may feel something of this about Edmund and Edgar. Edgar's first appearances in the play are brief and literally fleeting —he is twice shown being deceived by Edmund and then hastily escaping. He spends so much of the rest of the play in disguise that he does not at first seem to exist in his own right as a character, but to be used as a foil for Edmund, and as a help to the development of the other characters.

Edmund's first soliloquy gave us important clues to

his picture of the world, and the reason for his sense of deprivation. Edgar's first soliloquy does not tell us much about Edgar, but can almost be read as a sort of Greek chorus, commenting on the themes of the play. He is helpless, a beggar, 'near to beast', and must

> with presented nakedness outface
> The winds and persecutions of the sky. (II 3 11)

He paints a picture of a poverty-stricken countryside, without towns, where he may by lunacy 'enforce . . . charity'. Nakedness, exposure, unkind weather, suffering, madness—perhaps a people neglected by their ruler—he introduces these ideas in his speech, and perhaps more important, he 'presents Beggary' to the audience, actually shows them what a mad, naked beggar looks like.

Edgar's pitiable state as a Tom o' Bedlam wakes charity in Lear, and it is this naked madman whom the king adopts as his philosopher to answer his questions about the nature of the universe, and as his 'justicer' to judge his daughters. But Lear's wits are already wandering, and there is a pathetic inadequacy about his accusation of Goneril: 'she kicked the poor king her father' (III 6 47). And when Lear asks the vital question about Regan, 'Is there any cause in nature that makes these hard hearts?' (III 6 76), he does not stay for an answer, but withdraws into an imaginary bed, and lapses into sleep.

Edgar's later soliloquies are also used as choruses, to point morals, rather than to disclose his own feelings. Deeply significant and central to the play's meaning is the development following Edgar's assumption that he is now

> the *worst*,
> The *lowest* and *most* dejected thing of Fortune, (IV 1 2)

and that things must therefore improve. Meeting his blinded father he realises

Who is't can say 'I am at the worst'?
I am worse than e'er I was . . . .
And worse I may be yet: the worst is not
So long as we can say, 'This is the worst'. (IV 1 25)

Like Cordelia, he returns good for evil, saving his father both from suicide and capture. But once again we find Edgar used mainly, it seems, to further the plot, to disclose the wickedness of Goneril and Edmund to Albany, and later to tell Albany (and the audience) what has happened to Gloucester and Kent. Edgar destroys Edmund, and again draws a moral:

The gods are just, and of our pleasant vices
Make instruments to plague us. (V 3 169)

Good has defeated evil: Gloucester's blindness was a just punishment for his fornication. But this is by no means the full meaning of the play; life does not work out evenly and justly. Edgar arrives too late to save Cordelia, whose fate is by no means an illustration of natural justice.

The final words of the play are ambiguous and troubling rather than confident:

The oldest have borne most: we that are young
Shall never see so much, nor live so long.

'The oldest'—the play is not the tragedy of the children, tragic though the fates of four of them are, but of the fathers. And Gloucester at first seems not at all a tragic hero. He is shown as a good-humoured but insensitive man, fussy and upset when things turn out unexpectedly, or go wrong. The story requires him to be stupid and imperceptive enough to be easily hoodwinked by Edmund's implausible plot, though it appears much less plausible to the reader than it does to the audience in the theatre. Gloucester, already disturbed by the king's fantastic behaviour, and now deeply wounded by the idea that Edgar could be disloyal, falls an easy prey to Edmund's scheming.

Gloucester is a weak man, inclined to obey authority. He is sorry for Kent in the stocks, and shocked that the king's servant and representative should be treated in this way, but 'tis the Duke's pleasure' (II 2 149), and it would be uncomfortable and even dangerous to interfere. Yet Gloucester declares, 'I'll entreat for thee' (II 2 151). Torn between Lear, who has rightful authority but no power, and Cornwall who has power but no rightful authority to behave as he is doing, Gloucester can only say with conscious futility, 'I would have all well betwixt you' (II 4 116).

We see Gloucester shocked by Lear's being driven out into the storm, yet afraid to go to his assistance. It would be easy to do what Cornwall advises—'Shut up your doors, my lord; . . . Come out o'the storm' (II 4 304). This is the sort of practical, respectable advice we might expect Gloucester to take.

But he does not like 'this unnatural dealing' (III 3 1) and, ethics apart, he has heard secretly that 'a power' is 'already footed' (III 3 13) to avenge the king. Finally loyalty to what he feels is the right and natural state of affairs triumphs: 'If I die for it (as no less is threatened me) the King, my old master, must be relieved' (III 3 17).

What happens to Gloucester—and it happens, ironically, as the direct result of his loyalty and kindness—may to a modern audience seem worse than death. Dr. Johnson remarked that 'the extrusion of Gloucester's eyes seems an act too horrid to be endured in dramatic exhibition'. But we should remember that the Jacobean audience were accustomed not only to bull and bear-baiting—'I am tied to th'stake, and I must stand the course' (III 7 53) cries Gloucester—but to public executions, when the hangman customarily disembowelled his half-strangled victims—'these hangman's hands' of Macbeth's are dripping with blood. (II 2 29)

Gloucester's ordered world completely collapses. The king abdicates; nobles behave basely; guests assault a host; a son betrays his father. Only the poor—servants and an old tenant on his estate—display courage and kindness. And Gloucester does not realise that the naked beggar who rescues him—'when madmen lead the blind' (V 1 46)—is in fact re-establishing the 'natural' order in which a son respects and assists his father.

'I stumbled when I saw' (IV 1 19) says Gloucester; now, physically blinded, he perceives the truth. When he hears of the defeat of Lear and Cordelia, at first he refuses to go on. This is too much. But Edgar commands him:

> Men must endure
> Their going hence, even as their coming hither;
> Ripeness is all. Come on. (V 2 10)

And Gloucester seems to agree that 'ripeness' can only be attained through suffering and endurance of suffering. 'And that's true, too,' are the last words we hear him speak.

Questions:

1. Is Gloucester's fate, to any extent, his own fault?
2. Do you have any clear picture of Edgar's character?
3. Compare some of Edmund's speeches and attitudes with those of Shakespeare's earlier 'Machiavel', Richard III. Read 3 *Henry VI*, V 6 68–83 (Gloucester will become Richard III) and *Richard III*, I 1 14–41 and

I 3 324–338. How, if at all, does Shakespeare show sympathy with Edmund? Is there anything to be said for Edmund?

4. What does the subplot add to *King Lear*? How much would be lost if the Gloucester family was omitted from the play?

HOW THE PLAY IS WRITTEN

Shakespeare's text cannot be paraphrased. If we try to express in our own words what is said in any of the great speeches in *King Lear*, we will find that the effect of reading the two versions is completely different. We cannot separate matter from the manner of expressing it. Nevertheless we can look at various aspects of the prose and the poetry, one at a time, as long as we remember that it is the total experience of reading and hearing that is important.

We may when reading the poetry of *King Lear* notice in particular: first the movement of the verse, the rhythm, the beat; then in both poetry and prose, the language used, the kind of words, elaborate or simple, far-fetched or homely, scholarly or conversational; finally the images, or pictures, called up in our minds by the words.

People are apt to think of 'blank verse' as regular lines going 'ti-tum, ti-tum, ti-tum, ti-tum, ti-tum'. Some of Shakespeare's early work is in this regular pattern, with the pauses in the sense coming usually at the end of a line, but by the time he wrote *King Lear* he was writing with complete freedom—this beat is like the underlying rhythm section over which the players improvise at will. For instance, Lear's

Never, never, never, never, never. (V 3 308)

('tum-ti' five times) completely reverses the usual pattern. Shakespeare is writing the poetry of *King Lear* not line by line, but in paragraphs. In his earlier plays some characters spoke rhyming couplets, stanzas and even sonnets. Now Shakespeare has almost abandoned rhyme, except when necessary to create an air of formality (I 1 253–264), to round off a scene (I 2, IV 4) or to emphasise a moral (I 4 346–7).

Prose and verse are used, as and when they are the best vehicles for the meaning, with equal expressiveness and facility. When Lear finds Kent in the stocks, the regular movement of the King's authoritative speech is interrupted, first by the Fool's chatter (II 4 7–9) and then by Lear's exclamations of disbelief and horror and Kent's brief, echoing affirmations (II 4 14–20). Then Lear's dignified protest finds fit expression once more in regular rhythm.

The main part of the first scene of the play, written in stately ritualistic verse suitable for such a formal, public trial, is enclosed by two passages of prose: the first, casual chat showing us Gloucester's frame of mind and Edmund's position, the second showing the close understanding between Goneril and Regan, their real feelings and their low opinion of their father.

The Fool's usual utterance is either the back-chat, or the quick chatter, of the professional comedian. Kent says of a song, 'This is nothing, fool', and the Fool comes back at once with 'Then 'tis like the breath of an unfeed lawyer—you gave me nothing for't'. (I 4 129) Or he runs on:

> I marvel what kin thou and thy daughters are: they'll have me whipped for speaking true, thou'lt have me whipped for lying; and sometimes I am whipped for holding my peace. I had rather be any kind of thing than a fool: and yet I would not be thee, nuncle; thou hast pared thy wit o' both sides and left nothing i'th' middle. Here comes one o'the parings. *Enter Goneril* (I 4 182)

But notice how, speaking apparently lightly, he yet poses a central question of the play: 'what kin thou and thy daughters are'. His talk is 'full of wise saws and modern instances' (*As You Like It* II 7 156) and laced with proverbial wisdom:

> Truth's a dog must to kennel; he must be whipped out, when the Lady's brach may stand by th'fire and stink. (I 4 112)

Often the Fool bursts into snatches of song—many of them highly relevant to what is happening—and this is an indirect, and therefore a safer way to comment on the doings of his superiors.

In short, in this play Shakespeare uses whatever kind of writing is most effective, dramatically, at any particular point in the play. He uses extremes of style. Sometimes, as in Lear's speech at III 2 1 ff., Shakespeare piles enormous words and phrases upon each other, creating new combinations of words and extravagant images—thought-executing fires, oak-cleaving thunderbolts, the thick rotundity o' the world. But after the wind and the earthquake comes the still small voice. Perhaps the most moving, as certainly the simplest, speech in the play is Cordelia's response when the bewildered Lear marvels:

> I think this lady
> To be my child, Cordelia— (IV 7 69)

and she replies, 'And so I am, I am.' (It seems odd that Tate felt compelled to replace this by 'O my dear, dear Father'.) So quiet is Cordelia's manner of speech that she might well be described in the words Coriolanus used of his wife, 'my gracious silence'. (II 1 194)

Simplicity and brevity mark many of the key speeches. 'Who is it that can tell me who I am?' (I 4 230) cries Lear. Gloucester, now blind, admits 'I stumbled when I saw' (IV 1 19). Edgar raises his father after his mock suicide:

> Give me your arm.
> Up; so. How is't? Feel you your legs? You stand.

And Gloucester replies only 'Too well, too well' (IV 6 66). The cadence is that of Cordelia's reassurance to Lear, 'No cause, no cause' (IV 7 77).

The essential starkness of the play is both created and reflected by this plain language and by such simple repetition. A keyword may be repeated over and over again in a speech, as Edmund repeats 'base', 'bastard' and 'legitimate' (I 2 6–22). Or it may echo from scene to scene, as 'nothing' is dwelt upon by Lear and Cordelia (I 1 85 ff.), by Edmund and Gloucester (I 2 32 ff.) and by Kent, the Fool and Lear (I 4 131 ff.).

Repetition intensifies both Lear's anger with Oswald:

> O you sir, you, come you hither, sir. Who am I, sir?
> (I 4 79)

and Lear's final repetitions—'Howl, howl, howl' and

> Never, never, never, never, never.

Notice how the key-words, 'need', 'nature', 'patience', brought together at II 4 260–7, echo before and after throughout the play.

Shakespeare draws comparisons and makes pictures, or images, for us, from everything under the sun. You will often find the images in a particular play continually drawn from one or two particular things—in *Romeo and Juliet* from brief flashes of light, in *Troilus and Cressida* from food, over-eating and disease. Whether Shakespeare chose to do this consciously, or whether these were the comparisons that sprang spontaneously from his unconscious mind, we cannot know, but there is no doubt of their effect on the reader.

In *King Lear*, you are bound to notice how often there is reference to animals, often unpleasant animals. We have seen that 'naked unaccommodated man' is shown to be 'man brought near to beast'; and again, that a man who allows passion to master reason loses his rational soul, which is what distinguishes him from an animal. So Edgar talks of wicked man in animal terms: 'hog in sloth, fox in stealth, wolf in greediness, dog in madness, lion in prey' (III 4 92). Goneril is four times compared to a serpent, she has a wolfish visage, boarish fangs, she is a detested kite, she and Regan are pelican daughters, dog-hearted, she-foxes, tigers not daughters, and each an adder to the other. Worse still, 'Monster Ingratitude' (I 5 39) shapes Goneril in its own unnatural image; she is 'degenerate' (IV 2 43), less than human, less than animal, even. (See page 7). Her horrified husband uses such words as 'vile', 'filth', 'barbarous', 'devil', 'deformity', 'fiend' (IV 2 38–67) when speaking to her, and begs her 'Bemonster not thy feature!' (IV 2 63). He fears lest, following her example,

> Humanity must perforce prey on itself
> Like monsters of the deep, (IV 2 49)

and we are reminded of Ulysses' image of cannibalism as the last stage of anarchy, expressed in animal terms:

> And appetite, an universal wolf,
> So doubly seconded with will and power,
> Must make perforce an universal prey,
> And last eat up himself.
>
> (*Troilus and Cressida* I 3 121)

It is uncontrolled 'will and power' which have made Goneril a monster.

You will find continual references to eyesight, eyes, seeing, looking, beholding, blinding, throughout the whole play. These serve to emphasise another principal theme, that life must be looked at clearly, and seen truthfully. Goneril, exaggerating her love for Lear, values it 'dearer than eyesight' (I 1 54). Lear orders both Cordelia and Kent to avoid his sight (I 1 123, 156) and Kent implores him, 'See better, Lear' (I 1 157). Lear dreads Goneril's 'scornful' and 'fierce' eyes (II 4 161, 168), and hopes that Regan's will 'comfort and not burn' (II 4 169). Gloucester fears lest Regan's 'cruel nails' will 'pluck out' Lear's 'poor old eyes' (III 7 55); because Gloucester says that he 'shall see' vengeance overtake Lear's wicked children (III 4 64) Cornwall literally blinds him. When Lear meets the eyeless Gloucester, with horrible irony he claims to 'remember his eyes well enough' (IV 6 136) and they go on to pun and to jest bitterly about Gloucester's blindness. Cordelia's 'washed eyes' (I 1 226) have always seen clearly; but Gloucester has to be blinded before he sees truly: 'I stumbled when I saw' (IV 1 19). Lear too in the end sees 'straight' in every sense (V 3 287) and dies begging the bystanders to 'Look there, look there!' These are only a fraction of the references you will find as you read.

References to cruelty, torture and execution abound. Lear's nature is 'wrenched' out of place by an 'engine' (I 4 269)—probably the rack. The Fool pictures the loyal follower of a man who is losing power, as being dragged at breakneck speed downhill by a great wheel—another instrument of torture (II 4 69). Gloucester is bound; first his beard and then his eyes are plucked out, and he compares himself to a wretched bear 'tied to th'stake' (III 7 53). The world seems to him to be governed by gods who delight in cruelty for its own sake:

> As flies to wanton boys are we to th'gods;
> They kill us for their sport. (IV 1 37)

These constant allusions culminate when to Kent it appears that Lear's death is a release from torture:

Vex not his ghost: O, let him pass; he hates him
That would upon the rack of this tough world
Stretch him out longer. (V 3 313)

Miss C. E. Spurgeon, in *Shakespeare's Imagery* pages 338–343, points out the great number of words in *King Lear* which relate to 'a human body in anguished movement', and so continually remind us of the prolonged suffering which is being undergone.

Let us look closely at the beginning of one particular scene, III 2, to which I referred on page 63. The Gentleman and Kent have already set the stage, talking of 'foul weather' (III 1 1) and of how the king,

Contending with the fretful elements,
Bids the wind blow the earth into the sea
Or swell the curlèd waters 'bove the main . . .
(III 1 4)

In the same spirit did Northumberland, all his schemes in disorder, his son dead, demand:

Let heaven kiss earth! now let not Nature's hand
Keep the wild flood confined! Let order die!
(2 *Henry IV*, I 1 153)

The universe is one and indivisible: disorder in the spiritual world must be echoed in the physical world; tempests in the mind must be reflected by tempests in the skies. All through the play Lear has assumed supernatural powers and has invoked the elements. 'Blasts and fogs upon thee!' (I 4 300) he cries to Goneril, and later begs the 'taking airs', the 'nimble lightnings' and the 'fen-sucked fogs' to afflict her (II 4 159–163). He has confidently appealed to the heavens to take his part (II 4 185 ff.). But now he has turned away his beloved and loving daughter, and has himself been turned out of doors by his remaining children. He enters, creating and invoking the storm, demanding the destruction of the whole disordered world.

> Blow, winds, and crack your cheeks! rage! blow!
> You cataracts and hurricanoes, spout
> Till you have drenched our steeples, drowned the cocks! (III 2 1)

The idea is an Elizabethan commonplace; Ulysses declared that if degree (rank and order) were removed, as it has been in *King Lear*,

> the bounded waters
> Should lift their bosoms higher than the shore
> And make a sop of all this solid globe.
> (*Troilus and Cressida*, I 3 111)

But Lear expresses this with extraordinary force and power. The winds are to 'crack' their cheeks—a violent and painful image. A cataract is an ungovernable body of water, and we know from *Troilus and Cressida* (V 2 168) that Shakespeare associated the hurricano with water-spouts and with dizzy clamour and fury—'furicano' was the alternative Elizabethan form of the word, a word brought by new adventurers from the West Indies. 'Spout' is forcefully onomatopoeic and has also the emphasis which falls on the last word of a line. This is not to be a mere flood, slowly rising till the highest earthly object, the weather-cock on the church steeple, is drowned, but a violent assault with twirling columns of water. It has been suggested that Lear has in mind Genesis vii 11 and is calling for a new Deluge to cleanse the earth.

The language becomes elaborate and highly compressed; whole paragraphs of meaning are condensed into a rare word or a new-minted phrase.

> You sulph'rous and thought-executing fires,

Vaunt-couriers of oak-cleaving thunderbolts,
Singe my white head! And thou, all-shaking
thunder,
Strike flat the thick rotundity o'th'world,
Crack Nature's moulds, all germens spill at once
That make ingrateful man! (III 2 5)

'Sulph'rous' suggests the stink of hell and the powers of darkness—a bold, contradictory word to apply to lightning. Dr. Johnson said that 'thought-executing' meant 'doing execution with rapidity equal to thought', and later editors concur or suggest 'executing the thought of Him who casts you'. But since 'oak-cleaving' means 'cleaving oaks', and 'all-shaking' means 'shaking all', it is surely possible that 'thought-executing' also may mean 'executing thoughts', not only in the sense of carrying them out, but of wiping them out, beheading or annihilating them. Is not Lear, in imploring the lightning to 'Singe my white head', begging the heavenly fires to wipe out his consciousness? And there may well be a suggestion of the purging and purifying qualities of fire.

The lightning gallops ahead of the thunder—vaunt-courier—as a herald to prepare for the coming of a great army, a power which will split the mightiest tree, the toughest wood. The catastrophe must be *all*-embracing, the thunder *all*-shaking. Every word is laden with overtones. A 'round' or circle was a common symbol for 'all', and now the round world, swelling like a womb in which Nature is shaping all manner of life, must be struck flat: *all* the seeds of *all* life must perish. Some measure of the strength of this passage may be obtained by reading Florizel's comparatively flat expression of the same idea in *The Winter's Tale*:

Let Nature crush the sides o'the earth together

And mar the seeds within. (IV 4 489)

There could not be a greater contrast to the majestic poetry of the king's invocation, creating the storm, demanding the destruction of the whole world, than the pathetic prose whimpering of the Fool, the ordinary man caught in both physical and metaphysical tempests.

O nuncle, court holy water in a dry house is better than this rain water out o' door. Good nuncle in; ask thy daughters blessing! Here's a night pities neither wise men nor fools.

The Fool uses a proverbial phrase; to give 'court holy water' meant to flatter, or fawn. And he emphasises the insignificance of man, of whatever status or kind, in the face of nature.

Lear is oblivious. Again we may compare two ways of expressing similar thoughts if we first read the song in *As You Like It*, 'Blow, blow thou winter wind' (II 7 174), and then continue:

Rumble thy bellyful! Spit, fire! spout, rain!
Not rain, wind, thunder, fire are my daughters.
I tax not you, you elements, with unkindness:
I never gave you kingdom, called you children;
You owe me no subscription. Then let fall
Your horrible pleasure. Here I stand your slave,
A poor, infirm, weak and despised old man:
But yet I call you servile ministers,
That will with two pernicious daughters join
Your high-engendered battles 'gainst a head
So old and white as this. O ho! 'tis foul.

Aristotle felt that two main elements of tragedy were terror and pity. Lear's first speech was one to terrify; now, in much more simple language, he evokes pity. A Jacobean medical text-book, comparing the little world of man with the universe, states that 'the rumblings of the guts, their rapping escapes, the huddled and redoubled belchings of the stomach, do represent the fashion and manner of all kinds of thunders'. In three words Lear suggests this, and the mightiness of the being whose rumbling guts are heard as thunder.

On page 6 I suggested the double meaning which 'unkindness' carries, which emphasises Lear's daughters' sin against nature. Lear submits to the power of the elements, which a moment ago he was commanding as servants, and in a magnificent paradox describes himself as 'poor, infirm, weak'. Yet instantly he turns on them, and abuses them for allying themselves with his daughters. He is anticipating his later speech to Kent, when he declares that

this tempest in my mind
Doth from my senses take all feeling else
Save what beats there—filial ingratitude! (III 4 12)

and this obsession is again illustrated when Lear insists that Tom o' Bedlam's state can only derive from his daughters—

Didst thou give all to thy daughters? . . .
What, has his daughters brought him to this pass? . . .
Nothing could have subdued nature
To such a lowness but his unkind daughters.
(III 4 48, 62, 69)

The audience have barely time to feel, certainly no time to accept Lear at his own—incomplete—valuation, when they are jarred by the Fool's jest and his snatch of obscene song which—if the meaning be disentangled—does reflect on Lear.

The codpiece that will house
Before the head has any,

The head and he shall louse
So beggars marry many.

'If a houseless man marry, he will end up a lousy beggar.' This seems the usual interpretation, but I venture to suggest that here yet again there is some allusion to the war in man between will and judgement—the codpiece signifying lust or desire, and the head intelligence.

The man that makes his toe
What he his heart should make
Shall of a corn cry woe
And turn his sleep to wake.

This seems a versification of the proverb, 'Set not at thy heart what should be at thy heel'. The man who puts an insignificant and painful part where a kind and sound one should be, will be kept awake with pain, that is, Goneril and Regan replaced Cordelia, to Lear's pain and woe.

Even now we have by no means fully explored this passage, but perhaps I have suggested some of its richness, which further rereading will enhance.

Why should we bother about the way in which the play is written? Because, I think, this is what makes it a great play.

We may not find that Lear, considered as a character, is sympathetic or attractive; the plot, considered by itself, seems crude, and even silly. If we wrote a prose paraphrase of the play (you might try this with some part of it that seems to you important) it would lose almost all its force. But when we see Shakespeare's *King Lear*, or read it, we are profoundly moved, and we are on Lear's side. We can reverse Wilfred Owen's famous remark, and say 'The Pity is in the Poetry'. *King Lear* is a great play because it is written in great poetry, and no one can explain exactly what that is.

Further Reading:

A. C. Bradley, *Shakespearian Tragedy*, pp. 266 ff.

C. E. Spurgeon, *Shakespeare's Imagery*, particularly pp. 338 ff.

Questions:

Choose a passage which you consider particularly important, or moving, or well-written, and read it carefully, aloud if possible. (Suggested passages: I 1 81–106, I 2 1–22, II 4 260–282, III 4 62–111, IV 6 149–186, IV 7 45–85). Consider the total dramatic effect, and how it is achieved. Examine the movement of the speeches, the language and the imagery. It may be helpful to look at parallel passages in other plays by Shakespeare.

NOTES ON ENGLISH LITERATURE

Chief Adviser: JOHN D. JUMP, *Professor of English Literature in the University of Manchester*

General Editor: W. H. MASON, *Sometime Senior English Master, The Manchester Grammar School*

1 **Macbeth** (Shakespeare)
JOHN HARVEY

2 **The Prologue** (Chaucer)
R. W. V. ELLIOTT, *Professor of English, Flinders University, South Australia*

3 **Murder in the Cathedral** (T. S. Eliot)
W. H. MASON

4 **Pride and Prejudice** (Austen)
J. DALGLISH, *Sometime Senior English Master, Tiffin School*

5 **Twelfth Night** (Shakespeare)
BARBARA HARDY, *Professor of English, Birkbeck College*

7 **Wuthering Heights** (Emily Brontë)
BARBARA HARDY

8 **The Mayor of Casterbridge** (Hardy)
G. G. URWIN, *Senior English Master, Sale Grammar School for Boys*

9 **Jane Eyre** (Charlotte Brontë)
BARBARA HARDY

10 **St. Joan** (Shaw)
W. H. MASON

11 **Nostromo** (Conrad)
C. B. COX, *Professor of English Literature, University of Manchester*

12 **Absalom and Achitophel** (Dryden)
W. GRAHAM, *Sometime Senior English Master, Dame Allan's Boys' School, Newcastle-upon-Tyne*

13 **The Rivals, The School for Scandal, The Critic** (Sheridan)
B. A. PHYTHIAN, *Langley Park School for Boys, Beckenham*

14 **King Lear** (Shakespeare)
HELEN MORRIS, *Principal Lecturer in English, Homerton College, Cambridge*

15 **A Passage to India** (Forster)
W. H. MASON

Notes on English Literature

16 **The Nun's Priest's Tale and the Pardoner's Tale** (Chaucer)
R. W. V. ELLIOTT

17 **Paradise Lost, Books IV and IX** (Milton)
W. GRAHAM

18 **King Richard II** (Shakespeare)
HELEN MORRIS

19 **Men and Women** (Browning)
MARK ROBERTS, *Professor of English Literature, University of Belfast*

20 **The White Devil, The Duchess of Malfi** (Webster)
JOHN D. JUMP, *Professor of English Literature, University of Manchester*

21 **Middlemarch** (George Eliot)
A. O. COCKSHUT, *Fellow of Hertford College, Oxford*

22 **The Winter's Tale** (Shakespeare)
G. P. FOX, *Lecturer in English, Department of Education, University of Exeter*

23 **Sons and Lovers** (Lawrence)
CHRISTOPHER HANSON, *Lecturer in English Literature, University of Manchester*

24 **Sylvia's Lovers** (Mrs. Gaskell)
GRAHAM HANDLEY, *Senior Lecturer in English, All Saints' College Tottenham*

25 **Antony and Cleopatra** (Shakespeare)
HELEN MORRIS

26 **The Prelude I & II** (Wordsworth)
W. GRAHAM

27 **Howards End** (Forster)
G. P. WAKEFIELD, *Senior English Master, King George V School, Southport*

28 **Persuasion** (Austen)
J. R. COATES, *Senior English Master, Hymer's College, Kingston-upon-Hull*

29 **To the Lighthouse** (Woolf)
W. A. DAVENPORT, *Lecturer in English, Royal Holloway College*

30 **Man and Superman** (Shaw)
A. W. ENGLAND, *Senior Lecturer in English, Eaton Hall College of Education, Retford, Notts.*

31 **Riders to the Sea, Playboy of the Western World** (Synge)
A. PRICE

32 **Childe Harold III and IV, Vision of Judgement** (Byron)
PATRICIA BALL, *Lecturer in English, Royal Holloway College*

33 **Othello** (Shakespeare)
G. P. WAKEFIELD

34 **Bleak House** (Dickens)
P. DANIEL, *Assistant Master, Ratcliffe College, Leicester*

35 **Hard Times** (Dickens)
GRAHAM HANDLEY

36 **Death of a Salesman** (Miller)
C. J. PARTRIDGE, *Assistant Professor, Department of English Literature and Language, University of Victoria, B.C., Canada*

37 **Hamlet** (Shakespeare)
KEITH SAGAR, *Staff Tutor, Extra Mural Dept., University of Manchester*

38 **The Poetry of Gerard Manley Hopkins** (Hopkins)
H. C. SHERWOOD, *Senior Staff Tutor, Extra Mural Dept., University of Manchester*

39 **Paradise Lost I & II** (Milton)
W. RUDDICK, *Lecturer in English Literature, University of Manchester*

40 **Brighton Rock** (Greene)
A. PRICE

41 **A Portrait of the Artist as a Young Man** (Joyce)
CHRISTOPHER HANSON

42 **Lord Jim** (Conrad)
D. L. MENSFORTH

43 **Mansfield Park** (Austen)
R. A. COX, *Assistant Master, Manchester Grammar School*

44 **Coriolanus** (Shakespeare)
C. J. PARTRIDGE

45 **Romeo and Juliet** (Shakespeare)
HELEN MORRIS

46 **Volpone and The Alchemist** (Jonson)
MAURICE VENABLES, *Senior Lecturer in English, Redland College, Bristol*

47 **Tess of the D'Urbervilles** (Hardy)
JULIET MCLAUCHLAN, *Teacher of English, Aylesbury High School*

48 **Julius Caesar** (Shakesperare)
D. L. HIRST, *Lecturer in English, North Western Polytechnic, London*

49 **The Crucible** (Miller)
C. J. PARTRIDGE

50 **The Prioress's Tale & The Wife of Bath's Tale** (Chaucer)
M. PITTOCK, *Department of English, University of Aberdeen*